Retriever Training Drills for Blind Retrieves

JAMES B. SPENCER

Alpine
Blue Ribbon Books
Loveland, Colorado

Retriever Training Drills for Blind Retrieves
Copyright © 2001 by James B. Spencer

Library of Congress Cataloging-in-Publication Data

Spencer, James B.
    Retriever training drills for blind retrieves / James B. Spencer.
       p. cm.
    ISBN 1-57779-033-2
    1. Retrievers--Training. I. Title

SF429.R4 S628 2001
636.752'735--dc21   2001022721

Cover Photo: Theresa Spencer
Photos: James B. and Theresa Spencer
Editing: B. J. McKinney
Layout: Sharon Anderson
Cover Design: Laura Claassen

This book is available at special quantity discounts for breeders and for club promotions, premiums, or educational use. Write for details.

First printing October 2001

1 2 3 4 5 6 7 8 9 0

Printed in the United States of America.

Table of Contents

To Nancy Nieratko, who first suggested such a book—and
then kept reminding me of it.

Preface

This book is a companion to *Retriever Training Drills for Marking.* If you've already read that book, you can skip over to Chapter 2 and get ready to work on blind retrieves. But for those of you who are beginning with this book, perhaps I should explain the *raison d'être* for this multiple birth, especially to long-time readers of my work.

Frankly, at one time I thought I had already written all the retriever books I should. *Training Retrievers for Marshes & Meadows* explains how to train a retriever from puppyhood to finished dog status. *Retriever Training Tests* explains how to set up appropriate tests for training retrievers. And *Hunting Retrievers: Hindsights, Foresights, and Insights* describes the various retriever breeds and retriever dog-games. What else could one possibly say about retrievers? Nothing, I thought.

Then, a few years ago, I met Nancy Nieratko at a seminar I conducted in New Jersey. During lunch, and again at supper that evening—she and several other attendees dined with my wife and me—she bemoaned how difficult it is for a beginner to take a retriever from the Junior level to the Senior level in AKC hunting tests for retrievers. She told me that I should write a book to be titled *Getting to Senior.* Throughout these lamentations and entreaties, she used the word "drill" in almost every sentence. She mentioned, by name, many drills people use to advance their dogs, and pointed out that information about them is passed mostly by word of mouth, with almost nothing written down. Most beginners, she insisted, have no way to find out about these drills, at least at first. Further, she stressed, most beginners don't understand how necessary drilling—repetition, repetition, and more repetition—is for successful retriever training.

That rang a bell with me. In fact, a similar situation in the area of test design motivated my first book, *Retriever Training Tests.* But, like most writers, I instinctively resist book suggestions from others. So I gave Nancy my standard response: "If you think such a book should be written, why don't you write it yourself?" She demurred, saying she wasn't much of a writer, then went on to insist that such a book needed to be written.

By the time my wife and I were again home, I had all but dismissed the idea. I couldn't dispute Nancy's arguments, but I had no enthusiasm for such a project. Within a couple of weeks, I received a note from Nancy thanking me for the seminar—and again suggesting this book. "No way," I thought, "too much work!" (Someone long ago described writing a book as the "hardest work there is that doesn't involve heavy lifting.") Nancy and I repeated this stimulus/response sequence several times through the following few years, especially around holidays. She would send a card with a note suggesting the book. In a most non-Pavlovian way, my responses gradually weakened.

At length, I was "done in" by the enthusiasm of another woman, Joanne Carriera, who lives in Colorado and has never heard of Nancy Nieratko. In mid-1998, while she was doing an interview for a website for Alpine Publications, Inc., Joanne phoned me for information about myself and my books. After getting all the basic information, she asked—quite off-handedly, mostly to end the conversation politely—whether I had any ideas for future books. To my utter amazement, I heard myself blurting out, "Why, yes; I've been thinking of doing one about retriever training drills!"

With most website types—who, quite frankly, don't know which end of a dog to feed and which to clean up after—that would have passed almost unnoticed. However, Joanne is that rare website type who also "does" dogs. In fact, she has been heavily involved with herding dogs for years. Herding dog trainers drill their dogs as much as or perhaps even more than retriever trainers. (In fact, we "borrowed" the blind retrieve from herding trials.) So, the word "drills" clicked with her. She started asking intriguing questions, which I struggled to answer. We talked at length. Through this discussion, her contagious enthusiasm—for *any* book that would describe appropriate drills for beginners and convince them that they *must* drill their dogs—carried the day.

Next thing I knew I had a contract with Alpine to write a book to be titled *Retriever Training Drills*. Only after completing the second draft did I begin to suspect that I was working on two separate books. I wrote to Betty McKinney, Alpine's owner/publisher, saying, "I think I hear two heartbeats!" She studied my explanation and sent word to me through her Administrative Assistant, Sharon Anderson, that it was indeed twins and that I should proceed accordingly. Thus, *Retriever Training Drills* became *Retriever Training Drills for Marking* and *Retriever Training Drills for Blind Retrieves.*

THESE BOOKS ARE "AUXILIARY" TEXTS

Like *Retriever Training Tests*, these two books should supplement a complete training manual, such as *Training Retrievers for Marshes & Meadows*. The *Tests* book focuses on how to set up effective tests while following the *Marshes & Meadows* program. These two new books, *Drills for Marking* and *Drills for Blind Retrieves*, focus on the specific drills to use while following the *Marshes & Meadows* program.

THESE BOOKS EXPLAIN WHY

Like *Marshes & Meadows* and *Tests*, these two books tell you not only how, but also why.

When I started out in retrievers—back when the Roman Senator, Cato, was ending every speech with *"Carthago delenda est!"* (Carthage must be destroyed!)—I irritated several pros and not a few experienced amateurs with my incessant question, "Why should I do it that way?" I was seeking information, but they took my question as a challenge to the worth of whatever processes they were recommending. I've found that people who are totally wrapped up in dog training, especially of the "labor-intensive" retriever variety, tend to suffer a "process-oriented" form of tunnel blindness. They think only in terms of *how*, with little or no consideration of *why*. Of course, in anything as complex as retriever training, just figuring out the myriad of *how*'s is a daunting task. Consequently, retriever trainers, and especially pros, waste little of their time speculating about the associated *why*'s.

Frankly, that comes from long years of working with dogs, and therefore focussing entirely on canine mental processes. Pros can teach dogs only *how* to do this or that. They can't explain to dogs *why* they should do it. Would that it were otherwise! For example, it would be so nice if, before force-breaking a dog, a person could sit down with the beast and explain both what he is to do and why he needs this particular skill. You know, like you can do with a child. But dogs have nothing remotely approaching human intelligence.

People, on the other hand, are never completely comfortable with knowing only *how*. Rational intelligence craves information about *why*. In fact, curiosity about *why* starts at or before two years of age and continues until death. You may have heard the story about the man and his seven-year-old son walking down the street. The boy asked one question after another: "Why is the sky up?" . . . "Why can't penguins fly?" . . . "Why does it snow only in winter?" and so on. To each question, his father answered, "Beats me. I just don't know." Eventually, the boy asked, "Daddy, do you mind me asking all these questions?" The father replied, "Of course not, son. If you don't ask questions, how can you ever learn anything?"

Back when I started in retrievers, I often felt like that kid. I'd ask why, and get no answer, beyond an angry "Because it works!" By and large, I've had to work out my own *why*'s over the years—which has sometimes been a struggle. Thus, in my writing, I've always tried to share that information with my readers. I look at it this way: I write *about* dogs, but dogs can't read, so I must write *for* people—and people want to know *why*.

THESE BOOKS FOCUS ON FIELD WORK

Marshes & Meadows covers all phases of retriever training: puppy training, basic obedience, single marks, force-breaking, double marks, basic blind retrieves, advanced marks and blinds. Although each training phase requires drills of some kind, I've limited the drills in these two supplemental books to those involved in actual field work: single marks, double marks, triple marks, and blind retrieves. To keep these books reasonable in size, I've omitted the drills associated with puppy training, obedience, and force-breaking, all of which have received extensive coverage in many other texts. Not so field work drills. As Nancy Nieratko pointed out, most field drills are passed along by word of mouth, but have never been written down. Such written material as may exist is scattered through many sources, mostly magazine articles. Thus, in these two books, I've tried to bring together for the first time a comprehensive (although admittedly not exhaustive) collection.

THESE BOOKS ARE FOR AMATEURS
TRAINING THEIR OWN DOGS

In justice, I should point out that, in all likelihood, field trial pros developed almost every drill in this book. All of us who enjoy field work with retrievers owe practically everything we have—in the breeds themselves, in training techniques and equipment, and in basic dog-game formats—to field trialers, especially the highly talented and hard-working pros who have contributed so much, not only to field trials, but also to all other areas of retrieverdom.

However, in orienting this book to amateurs training their own dogs, I have necessarily had to focus on hunters and hunt test participants, not field trialers. Most hunters and over half of all hunt testers train their own dogs. This is not the case among field trialers. Almost none of the amateur field trialers trains his own dog. By "field trialers," I mean those who compete seriously and successfully in the major stakes, where championship points are awarded to the placing dogs. Field trials are so competitive that, for most participants, full-time professional training is the only rational road to success. Granted, a handful of wealthy amateurs who have unlimited leisure time and extensive training facilities do indeed train their own retrievers well enough to compete with the pros. (I do not include in this group those somewhat more numerous amateurs who "train their own dogs" under the direct and constant supervision of pros. By any reasonable standard, their dogs receive full-time professional training.) Thus, as I said, almost none of the amateur field trialers trains his own dogs. So writing a *training* book for field trialers would be foolish. (An appropriate book for aspiring field trialers would contain only a list of the names, addresses, and phone numbers of all the field trial pros across the country. That's all the information the novice field trialer needs—and the sooner he gets it, the sooner he will begin to win.) Since I've written this book for the hunter and hunt tester, not the field trialer, I've omitted those few drills that have little application outside of the esoteric field trial world.

Throughout this book, I've kept in mind the limitations under which most amateurs must train their own dogs for hunting and hunting tests. Few have ideal training grounds. Few have unlimited time. Few have unlimited discretionary spending money for equipment. Frankly, keeping such limits in mind has been easy, for I've been drilling my own dogs under similar circumstances for several decades! I would have had difficulty *not* identifying with all other such trainers!

1
Why Drill?

I've been told that angels have what is called "infused knowledge." That term presumably means that they received all the knowledge they have—which I've been told is considerable, at least when compared to that of human beings—without effort. They didn't have to memorize definitions and principles. They didn't have to work a seemingly endless series of problems. In fact, they didn't have to study in any way. They just *know*, period.

I've had no personal experience with angels, so I can only repeat here what I've heard about them. But I have had extensive experience with dogs over the past 45 years, and I have observed that dogs, too, have "infused knowledge" in a limited way. We breed them to do certain things naturally or, as we often say, instinctively. Hounds trail and tree fur naturally. Pointing breeds seek and point birds naturally. Spaniels quarter and flush birds naturally. Retrievers mark falls and retrieve naturally. And so on. Dogs do these things—and the above is by no means an exhaustive list of instinctive behaviors we have bred into the various types of dogs—with only the most elementary exposure to suitable opportunities. Given half a chance, nature will out.

Useful as these instinctive behaviors are to those of us who enjoy hunting with dogs, they are not sufficient in and of themselves to produce finished workers. Far from it. To turn a well-bred dog into the kind of worker we seek, we must complement his instinctive behavior with appropriate elements of "learned behavior," a.k.a. "training." How much training a given dog requires depends on what type he is and on how "polished" the boss wants him to be. Hounds require—and will accept— very little. If a hound avoids running trash, loads up on command, and comes in when called (provided he has nothing better to do), he's "well trained." Dogs from long-tailed pointing breeds (the Pointer and the three Setter breeds) require more training. They should maintain some sort of contact with their handlers, should be staunch on point (and perhaps steady to wing and shot), should back-point, should stop-to-flush, and should respond to basic obedience commands (*Whoa, Come, Heel*) under reasonable circumstances. For owners who insist on retrieving, they should also be force-broken. Dogs of the bob-tailed pointing breeds (the German Shorthair, Brittany, Weimaraner, Vizsla, German Wirehair, Wirehaired Pointing Griffon, and so on) require even more training than long-tailed pointing dogs, especially in range control and retrieving (which may or may not be natural to them). Dogs of the flushing spaniel breeds (English Springer, English Cocker, American Cocker, Welsh Springer, Clumber, Sussex, American Water Spaniel, and so on) require substantially more training than bob-tailed pointing breeds. They must quarter within gun range, turn on a whistle command, flush vigorously, and retrieve very well (which most of them do naturally) on land and in water. Ideally a spaniel should be steady, that is, it should *Hup* (sit) after flushing a bird, and remain in place until sent to retrieve or continue hunting. As you can see, as we move from hounds to pointing breeds to spaniels, the training requirements increase dramatically.

When we move from spaniels to retrievers, well, as Al Jolson used to say, "You ain't seen nothin' yet!" The training requirements for retrievers is at least an order of magnitude (ten times) greater than that of spaniels! A retriever must sit quietly by the blind until all the birds are down. He must ignore decoys. He must do multiple marked retrieves through all manner of natural hazards (wind direction, cover variations, terrain changes, and so forth). And, most importantly, he must do blind retrieves on land and in water. Nothing in the instincts of any dog inclines him to do blind retrieves naturally. Thus, the blind retrieve is totally trained, totally taught, as a complex mixture of three basic elements: lining, stopping, and casting. Although the blind retrieve alone makes retriever training much more "labor intensive" than spaniel training, the rest of retriever field training—namely, marked retrieving—also requires a lot of work, at least as much as it takes to fully train a spaniel. This book covers drills with which you can train your dog to do blind retrieves. (The companion volume, *Retriever Training Drills for Marking*, covers drills for marks.)

But before getting into the drills themselves, you should acquaint yourself with the underlying motivation for drilling as such. Only after you understand that can you maximize the benefits of the drills described in this book.

FOR PEOPLE: "REPETITIO EST MATER STUDIORUM"
("Repetition is the Mother of Learning Techniques")

This Latin proverb is traditionally mistranslated as "repetition is the mother of learning." Through dint of—you guessed it—repetition, this mistranslation has become widely accepted in our culture. It even rings with profound wisdom—because it is pithy, because it deals in some abstract way with "learning," and, of course, because it has been repeated so often.

Be that as it may, "repetition is the mother of learning" misses the point of this old Roman proverb—by mistranslating "*studiorum*" as "learning" instead of as some more accurate term, such as "studies," "efforts," "approaches," or (most accurate, in this particular case) "learning techniques." For the ancient Romans, this proverb proclaimed that, without repetition, no *approach* to learning could be effective. Although true for both physical and mental skills, it is more obviously so for the former. To acquire any physical skill, one must practice, practice, practice. In any sport, different coaches break their practice sessions down in different ways, but they all insist on seemingly endless repetitions of drills. In the early 1970s (as I recall), psychologists developed a new approach to the acquisition of physical skills, namely, "mental practice." In this technique, the student closes his eyes and visualizes mentally that he is performing the skill properly, and also visualizes the results. For example, a golfer pictures himself swinging a 5-iron correctly, and then visualizes the ball climbing crisply before falling on the green. Various experiments indicated that this could be 70 to 80 percent as effective as physical practice. Did this new learning technique sidestep, and therefore disprove, "*repetitio est mater studiorum*"? No way! Essential to the success of "mental practice" is, you guessed it, repetition! The person must repeat this exercise over and over for about 15 minutes each session, for several sessions a day, for several days before showing the promised improvement. (And, of course, he would improve still more if he spent the same amount of time hitting real golf balls.)

The acquisition of mental skills also requires repetition. Whether in mathematics, a physical science, a social science, a philosophic discipline, or whatever, the general learning process consists of the same two phases: The student learns and memorizes the basic definitions, principles, and methodologies; then he applies these to a series of "problems" (equations, experiments, situations, syllogisms, and so forth). Repetition is essential for both memorization and problem solving. Educators are forever developing (and abandoning) new approaches, new ways to present the material in this or that discipline. But, to be even minimally successful, each new approach must rely heavily on repetitions by the students. Thus, in human learning, whether physical or mental skills are involved, we can confidently state that, to be effective, every learning technique must be lovingly nursed at the bountiful breasts of "Mother Repetition."

FOR DOGS: "EXERCITATIO EST MATER STUDIORUM"
("*Drilling is the Mother of Training Techniques*")

If repetition is essential for human learning, how could it be less than essential for dog training? Dogs, after all, lack human intelligence. (If you doubt that, try teaching a dog to read and write!) Contrary to today's trendy canine psycho-babble, we train dogs—we always have and always will—through a process which Pavlov long ago named "conditioning." We teach a dog to respond in a certain way to a certain stimulus—for example, to sit on a single whistle blast—by making sitting the dog's "conditioned response" to the whistle blast stimulus. We can condition a dog thusly through various training techniques, some positive, some negative, some more, and some less effective. But, essential to the success of whatever techniques we use is—again you guessed it—repetition, and lots of it!

In common dog-training parlance, frequent repetition of specific training techniques is called "drilling." Thus, we train dogs through drilling. We drill them to bring out their natural instincts, and we drill them to teach them to perform tasks beyond their natural instincts. Over the years, dog trainers have developed better and better techniques, frequently as a result of improvements in equipment. However, the one constant through the entire history of dog training is, and always will be, *drilling*.

Drills prepare a retriever for hunting tests.

TRIAL-AND-SUCCESS—TRIAL-AND-ERROR

In general, you use a two-phased approach to training your dog in any skill. In the first phase, which I have long called "trial-and-success," you lead your dog through the stimulus/response sequence under circumstances in which he has almost no chance to make a mistake. Let's take sitting on the whistle as an example. With your puppy on lead, you toot the whistle as you push his rump to the ground with your left hand and hold his head up with the lead. As soon as he is sitting, you praise him (very important). You do this repeatedly until he begins to sit before you can push his rump down. In this phase, you have led him through the proper response and you have rewarded him (with praise—or even food treats, if you like). He now knows how he should respond to the *Sit*-whistle, but he doesn't yet understand that he *must* do it every time.

To teach him the *necessity* of sitting on command, you move into phase two, which I have long called "trial-and-error," in which you allow him to make mistakes and correct him each time he does. With the puppy still on lead, so you can control him, you toot the whistle when he is a little distracted. If he sits, you praise him. If he ignores the whistle, you tap him crisply on the rump, either with your hand or a "sit-stick." Although this should not be a heavy blow, he should feel it and find it unpleasant enough to be avoided in the future. This tap on the rump puts him in a sitting position—so you praise him (even more important after a correction). You repeat this with various distractions to tempt him to ignore the whistle. Gradually, he learns that not sitting on the whistle brings unpleasant consequences—just as sitting on the whistle brings pleasant consequences. Eventually, after you have given him enough of this trial-and-error work, he will sit automatically when you toot the whistle, no matter what.

To put it another way: In the trial-and-success phase, you teach your dog to "do good," in the trial-and-error phase, you teach him to "avoid evil." To be fully conditioned, he needs both. Trial-and-success, because of its rewards, gives your dog a positive attitude toward whatever command you are teaching him. Trial-and-error, because of its punishments, teaches him that he must obey, whether he feels like it or not. Both phases are necessary to completely condition your dog.

In recent years, a lot of ink has been splashed about advocating "totally positive reinforcement." Loosely translated, this means use only phase-one techniques, with their rewards, but never use phase-two techniques, with their punishments. This is pure psycho-babble. When your retriever is high-balling after a jack rabbit instead of carrying your line to a blind retrieve—and especially if the rabbit is heading toward a four-lane divided—you'll be glad you reinforced the *Sit*-whistle with the "*not* totally positive reinforcements" of the trial-and-error phase. Had you used only the "totally positive reinforcement" of the trial-and-success phase, he would almost certainly decide to forego whatever delights you might have in store for him this time. He would rather catch the rabbit.

When your retriever is properly conditioned—to stop on the whistle, or obey any other command—he will obey happily, because of phase-one drilling, but he will also have some fear of disobeying, because of phase-two drilling. To be reliable, he needs both. As the ancient Romans said: *"Verba sapientibus"* (words for the wise).

DRILL, BUT DON'T OVERWORK YOUR DOG!

I have stressed the necessity of drilling so much because so many beginners have difficulty believing it's really necessary. They seem to think that as soon as the dog does something right once, he is fully trained in that particular area. "Hey, let's move on to something new and exciting! Why mess around with what he already knows?" I've had to deal with this attitude in many of the beginners I have helped out. I have heard it in the seminars I have conducted and in the ones I have attended. Other experienced trainers have told me of similar experiences. In fact, when I first began working on this book, I asked two people, one in New Jersey, the other in Kansas, what they would recommend I include. Both are well past the beginner stage now, but not so far removed from it that they don't remember it quite clearly. I expected that each of them would request that I include this or that special drill. To my surprise, neither of them mentioned a specific drill. Instead, both of them—independently, for they don't even know each other—urged me to do everything I could to convince beginners that drilling is absolutely necessary.

But, having put so much stress on the necessity of drilling, I now fear that I may lead a very small minority of beginners into the mistaken notion that they should drill their dogs spraddle-legged in every training session. I've known a few such beginners. They are very intense, totally focussed, and a joy to work with, for they absorb everything you tell them like sponges—and can repeat it back to you word for word months later if necessary. Most of them stay in the sport a long time and become excellent trainers. However, they tend to take too much out of their dogs for many years (and many dogs). They do this not by overly negative training techniques but simply by too much drilling per training session, day in, day out, week in, week out, for years. Whenever such a person gets a dog out of his crate, the dog knows he will be totally exhausted before he gets any kind of rest. The dog learns to adapt his pace to the workload he knows he is facing. Instead of running, he walks. And, strangely enough, if the dog walks straight enough, this type of beginner doesn't seem to notice how slowly he is moving. In short, his first few dogs become very precise "pigs." (A "pig" is a retriever with no style.)

So, for the minority of beginners with such tendencies, let me caution against too much drilling per session. Every dog has a "magic number" for repetitions. That number may be three or it may be eight, but it will seldom be anything greater than eight. In one training session, repeat a drill up to the dog's magic number and he will continue to improve, and will maintain his style. Push him beyond it and he will either deliberately mess up (especially Chesapeakes), or he will slow his pace. A few do both.

It's up to the trainer to know his dog's magic number—and to respect it! You can determine your dog's magic number by watching both his performance and his style. When he begins to do a drill worse instead of better, or when he begins to slow down, you should realize that you have exceeded his magic number. Put him up immediately, and next time you get him out, reduce the number of repetitions accordingly.

If possible, train with a group. In a group, you take turns working and resting your dogs, which reduces the risk of overworking any one of them in any one session. If you can't train with a group as often as you should, consider training two or three dogs, so you can rotate them. If you train alone and have only one dog, you simply have to put him up for a rest and a drink of water at appropriate intervals. This is extremely difficult to do, I know. When you are standing around with no one to talk to while your dog resets his magic number counter, time hangs heavily on your hands. But just grit your teeth and remember that you want a stylish retriever, not a pig.

THE DRILLS IN THIS BOOK

In a very technical sense, this book contains not drills, but training procedures. Only you can turn them into drills—by running your dog through them repetitively. If you were to use each one of them only once before moving on, you would not be drilling your dog, and he would end up thoroughly confused, not thoroughly trained. On the other hand, if you drill him appropriately with them, he should become a retriever you can be proud of, and he will enjoy the process as much as you do. It's up to you—not me, and not your dog.

Some of the drills in this book are phase one, trial-and-success drills, intended to help you lead your dog through the proper response with minimal chance of error. Some of them are phase two, trial-and-error drills, intended to tempt your dog to make a mistake so you can correct him. Some of them combine phase one and phase two, in that they start out as phase one and then advance into phase two. As you study each drill, you will see where it fits in this two-phased approach.

This book does not—and could not—contain every drill used by retriever trainers. Even if it contained all of them as of today, by tomorrow it would be missing a few, for trainers all over the country are developing new ones regularly. However, this book does contain a representative set of drills, certainly enough to train a retriever to do everything retrievers are supposed to do, at least according to hunting test standards. Incidentally, as best I can recall, I invented only one of them! I won't indicate which one that is, lest I offend someone who may have also invented it independently. The rest of these drills I have picked up here and there over the past 45 years. I have identified the creator of each drill for which I have that information—which, unfortunately, is only a few of them.

Photo courtesy of Bobbie Christensen

2
An Overview of the Blind Retrieve

WHAT IS A BLIND RETRIEVE?

A "blind retrieve," or more simply a "blind"—called an "unseen" in England—is a retrieve in which the dog does not see the bird fall and therefore must be directed to it by his handler, typically with whistle commands, voice commands, and arm signals. Blind retrieves occur frequently in waterfowl hunting, especially when two or three hunters shoot several birds from the same flock. In such a situation, the dog seldom sees every bird fall. Blinds can also happen when a duck hunter drops a bird in one direction while his dog is off retrieving another bird in a different direction. Blind retrieves also occur in upland hunting, although less frequently than in waterfowling. For example, a dog can flush a pheasant from cover so tall and heavy that he can't see the bird as it flies away. If the hunter knocks the bird down, his dog will have no idea where it fell. In many such situations, the hunter can simply walk his dog to the area of the fall and have him "hunt 'em up." But if the bird fell on the far side of a stream too wide for the hunter to jump and too deep for him to wade comfortably, he should have his dog pick it up as a blind. If you've hunted very many years, you can remember any number of situations, in both waterfowling and the uplands, in which blind retrieves have come up.

To pick up such a bird, a dog must have been trained to "handle," that is, to perform the three parts of a blind retrieve: *line*, *stop*, and *cast*. The handler *lines* his dog when he initially sends him from his side in the direction of the unseen bird. A dog that lines well will carry that line a reasonable distance without veering off. However, various hazards

11

Casting. Photo by Theresa Spencer.

(wind, terrain, and cover) may eventually throw him off-line so that he is no longer on a collision course with the bird. When that happens, the handler blows the *Sit*-whistle (also called the *Stop*-whistle), which is typically a single sharp blast on the whistle (*Tweeet!*). The properly trained retriever then stops, turns to face the handler, and sits down, awaiting redirection. (In water, he turns and looks at the handler while continuing to paddle around enough to keep from sinking.) The handler then gives his dog a *cast*, typically with an arm signal accompanied by either a whistle or voice command. The dog then runs or swims in the direction of that cast until he either finds the bird or hears the *Sit*-whistle again. And so on, until the dog picks up the bird.

In a blind retrieve, the handler controls the dog all the way to the bird. He doesn't just turn the critter loose to run wild, hoping he will eventually stumble on the bird. No, in a blind retrieve, the handler keeps his dog reasonably close to the true line to the bird all the way. He controls him this rigorously for a couple of very good reasons. First, the dog will get to the bird more quickly. And second, the dog won't disturb cover unnecessarily. This latter is especially important, for a dog that disturbs too much cover can flush birds out of gun range.

HOW THE BLIND RETRIEVE STARTED

Dave Elliot, a professional retriever trainer in Scotland, invented the blind retrieve, probably shortly after World War I. He told the entire story in his (out-of-print) book, *Training Gun Dogs to Retrieve* (Holt, NY, 1952)—but he managed to tell it in considerable detail without ever mentioning when it happened! (He also tells the story of his life from birth until he became a professional trainer without mentioning any dates!) I know from another source that he came to this country in 1931. But long before coming here, he was famous throughout British retriever field trial circles for having invented the blind retrieve. In fact, it was mostly because of his fame in the British Isles that the American Jay Carlisle brought him to this country in 1931 to manage his Labrador kennel and train his dogs. World War I must have interrupted field trials throughout the British Isles, so I've concluded that he invented the blind retrieve early in the 1920s.

Whenever it was, he did this by attending a stock dog trial in Scotland on his day off. At that trial, he watched handlers direct their dogs with whistle and arm signals as they herded livestock through chutes and so forth. It occurred to Dave that, if he could train his retrievers that way, he would be able to win more field trials. He would not only pick up more birds but also be able to "wipe eyes." In British field trials, several dogs are under judgment simultaneously, with driven birds falling here, there, and everywhere. If a judge tells one handler to retrieve a particular bird, and his dog fails to find it, the judge asks another handler to "have a go at it." If the second handler's dog succeeds, he is said to have "wiped the eye" of the other (unsuccessful) handler.

Dave tried training his retrievers to take whistle and arm signals— and it worked. Consequently, he began to win so many field trials that he became quite famous as a trainer. During the 1920s members of the American economic aristocracy began to travel to England to hunt with British nobility. They were thus exposed to the talents of Labrador retrievers, which they began to import into this country. They imported not only the dogs, but also their trainers. Jay Carlisle grabbed the brass ring, so to speak, when he brought Dave Elliot over here. Mr. Carlisle and Dave Elliot contributed greatly to the development of the American field trial format, which the American Kennel Club accepted and began sponsoring in 1932. Thus, the blind retrieve has been a major part of our trials and tests ever since.

TOTALLY TRAINED

Nothing in a retriever's genes inclines him to do blind retrieves. We can't breed them to line, stop, and cast instinctively. (Nor can stock-dog breeders, for that matter.) No, the blind retrieve is totally trained. We must drill all three parts (lining, stopping, and casting) into the dog until they become conditioned responses.

We first drill each of the three parts separately. Thus we have lining drills, stopping drills, and casting drills. Since blind retrieves occur both on land and in water, we must drill our retrievers in lining, stopping, and casting in both elements. Not surprisingly, we drill on land first and in water only after the dog is well along on land. Then, after the dog has mastered each part separately, we introduce him to drills that combine the parts. Finally, we take him through drills that help him make the transition to real blind retrieves.

In this book, separate chapters are devoted to drills for lining on land, lining in water, stopping (land and water), casting (land and water), combination drills (land and water), suction drills (land and water), and transition (to real blind retrieves) drills. In general, you can start drilling your dog on all three parts of the blind retrieve (lining, stopping, and casting) simultaneously on land. "Simultaneous," however, doesn't mean "in combination with one another." It means *separately but in the same training sessions*. After your dog lines, stops, and casts acceptably on land, you can advance him into drills that combine the parts. You can also begin lining drills in water while simultaneously introducing a separate drill to combine stopping and casting in water. And so on. Then you can begin to work on the suction drills. Finally, you take your dog through transition drills to help him make the leap from drills to real blind retrieves.

However, don't bother trying to hurry through any part of this training. I say "don't bother" because you can't do it even if you try. You see, *you will be drilling your dog in these basic skills all through his active life*. You'll never stop using the first lining drill you teach him (either the "Visual Aid Pattern Blind" or the "Modern Sight Blind," whichever you prefer). Nor will you ever stop using most of the other drills in this book.

In marking, which is in your retriever's genes, you use certain drills to bring out his natural abilities and certain other drills to instill control (like angles in water). Thereafter, you "coast" through the rest of his life by running your dog on more and more advanced real marked retrieves, not drills. Such is not the case in the blind retrieve. No, you must drill him in lining, stopping, and casting—individually and in combination—all his active life. For this reason, I've long thought the best trainer background for the blind retrieve is formal obedience trial competition. In obedience, as in the blind retrieve, every move is drilled in; nothing is bred into the dog's genes. Thus those who compete successfully in obedience trials understand the need to drill their dogs on the same things for life. (However, some of them have a little trouble giving their dogs enough freedom to learn to mark on their own.)

So, as you introduce your dog to these drills, remember that most of them will be with you for the life of your dog. That way, you won't be tempted to rush through them the first time.

3
Lining
Concepts

TO OR FROM?

In a blind retrieve, when your retriever leaves your side on command and runs in the direction you have indicated, he is "lining," or "taking a line." He is also operating on blind faith. He has seen nothing fall, so has no "personal" knowledge that a bird lies somewhere out there in that general direction. He is taking your word for it. After he has succeeded in finding birds this way many times, he has good reason to believe you. But when you first begin to train him to line, he has no reason at all to leave your side. Thus, you must provide the initial motivation, which you can do in only two ways: You can teach him to run *to* something (a reward), or you can teach him to run *from* something (a punishment).

If you introduce your dog to lining with drills that teach him to run *to* something, he'll *want* to take your line, and he's more likely to succeed every time. Consequently, he'll run happily, with all the style and *élan* his genes allow. He'll enjoy the training and make excellent progress. After running enough such drills, he'll be so conditioned to running long and straight lines that he'll do it in real blind retrieves—and he'll run them with enthusiasm.

On the other hand, if you introduce your dog to lining with drills that teach him to run *from* punishment, his attitude will show it. Even if you drive him to run rapidly, he'll run with his tail tucked under and his ears laid back. In the vocabulary of retrieverdom, "style" and "speed" are not interchangeable terms. Some who train their dogs to run *from* punishment have developed techniques for generating speed in their dogs, but that's a poor substitute for the style they have killed.

This is not to say that running *from* punishment has no place in teaching a retriever to line. As in almost all phases of training, after you teach your dog what you expect with trial-and-success drills, you must introduce at least a little trial-and-error work to convince him that, if he doesn't perform properly, you can and will visit sundry unpleasantries upon him. But that comes later. Initially, you should rely exclusively on positive motivation, which will both teach him what you want him to do and encourage him to enjoy doing it.

The author prepares to line Beaver to a visual aid across the pond.

THE "PICTURE" CONCEPT

If someone were to ask you to walk, say, 100 steps in a particular direction, would you stare at your feet as you walked? Of course not! You would select some distant object in the indicated direction and walk

After being sent, Beaver swims straight at the visual aid.

toward it, watching it constantly as you did. That's approximately what an experienced retriever does in a blind retrieve. At the line, he looks in the direction the boss indicates. He selects the spot he thinks most likely to hold the bird. When sent, he'll run straight to that spot. Retriever folks refer to that spot as the dog's "picture." How does a dog select a picture? He recalls previous retrieves (blinds and marks) that he's made in similar situations, and selects the one that seems most appropriate for the scenery currently before him. I've long called this process "looking through his picture album." He has stored pictures of past retrieves in his memory, and he uses them as a guide for the current blind retrieve. The more pictures he has in his album, the higher the probability that he'll select a suitable one for any given blind retrieve.

A "picture" gives a retriever something to run *to*. Thus, you should encourage your dog to paste pictures in his album from the very beginning of his training in lining. You do this by selecting drills that encourage pictures, especially at first. Chapter 4, "Lining Drills for Land," and Chapter 5, "Lining Drills for Water," contain some drills that encourage pictures and some that don't. In general, drills identified as "trial-and-success" are "picture" drills, while drills identified as "trial-and-error" are not.

THE "FAIRWAY" CONCEPT

As was explained in Chapter 2, a blind retrieve is a *controlled* retrieve. It is not a random romp with—you hope—a "surprise-surprise!" happy ending. In dog-games, the judges set up blind retrieves specifically to test your control over your dog under challenging conditions. They expect you to keep your dog reasonably close to the true line to the bird from the time he leaves your side until he picks up the bird. A dog that runs close enough to the true line is said to be "within the fairway." The dog that drifts out of the fairway disturbs cover unnecessarily and could flush birds out of gun range while there.

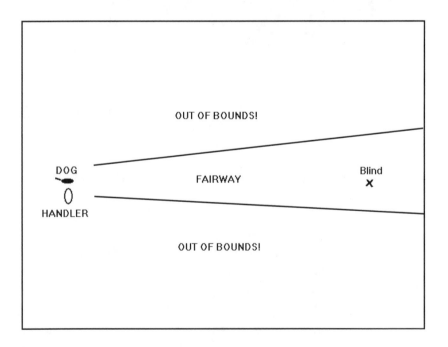

Figure 1. Fairway Concept.

Even in hunting, when you have only yourself to please, you shouldn't let your dog disturb cover unnecessarily on his way to blind retrieves. The more cover he runs through, the greater the risk he'll flush a bird out of gun range. Not only will you have no chance to shoot that bird, but also your out-of-control dog will almost certainly chase it into the next county, perhaps flushing and chasing still other birds as he does. Clearly, you should keep your dog within a reasonable fairway in hunting, too.

How wide should a "reasonable" fairway be? To help define it, let's rely on a related concept that has long been well defined, namely, the "area of the fall" for a mark. When hunting for a marked retrieve, the dog needs some "geography" around the bird in which to hunt. No dog can consistently pin his marks, especially when they are long and fraught with terrain and cover hazards. The area in which he can be reasonably allowed to hunt is called "the area of the fall." If he fails to stay within that area, he is said to disturb too much cover. Now, since both concepts ("area of the fall" and "fairway") define when a dog is and is not disturbing too much cover, would it be too outrageous to suggest that they

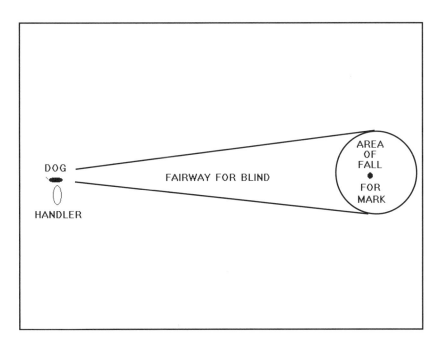

Figure 2. Relationship Between Fairway of a Blind Retrieve and Area of the Fall of a Mark.

share a common width near the bird? *Au contraire!* To suggest anything else would outrage common sense!

As is explained in the companion volume, *Retriever Training Drills for Marking,* retrieverites have long defined the area of the fall as "a circle around the bird, the diameter of which is approximately 20 percent of the distance from the line (the place from which the handler initially sent the dog) to the bird". Thus, the area of the fall for a 50-yard mark would be a circle around the bird with a diameter of about 10 yards; for a 75-yard mark it would be a 15-yard circle; for a 100-yard mark, a 20-yard circle; and so on.

If, on a mark, a dog within that 20 percent circle is not disturbing too much cover, by what curious logic could anyone claim that the same dog within the same circle would be disturbing too much cover if the same bird were not a mark, but a blind retrieve? Whether the dog saw the bird fall or not, cover is cover, and the dog either disturbs too much of it or he doesn't. Thus, we may reasonably assume that, near the bird, the width of the fairway for a blind retrieve is identical to the width of the "area of the fall" for the same bird as a mark: 10 yards wide for a 50-yard blind, 15 yards wide for a 75-yard blind, 20 yards wide for a 100-yard blind, and so on.

Of course, the fairway cannot be the same width all the way from the line to the bird. It should start very narrow, almost a point, at the line and widen as it goes out toward the bird. Thus, the fairway is cone-shaped, with the cone's point at the line and the wide end out where the bird lies.

(*Non-trivial corollary*: On a mark, the dog should have the same cone-shaped path to the bird as he would have if it were a blind retrieve. Common sense demands that the dog be given the same leeway to and around the bird whether or not he saw it fall.)

So much for geometry. As you will learn from hanging around with retriever people, "real world" practical definitions are almost never this precise. Sure, anyone with a reasonable amount of experience will agree that the area of the fall is a circle with a diameter about 20 percent of the distance from the line to the bird. But, then, everyone (myself included) will begin to hedge. "Of course, that is only an initial approximation, which must be adjusted up or down depending on conditions." In estimating the area of the fall for any particular mark, we try to allow the dog a reasonable amount of geography in which to hunt without being penalized for a loose hunt. Thus, the area would be larger for the last bird in a triple mark than for the same bird as the go-bird, for obvious reasons. Terrain, cover, and wind conditions can increase or decrease the area of the fall. But, all of our cherished hedges affect the final area of the fall only slightly.

So this 20 percent rule is a good working measure, especially for beginners who need something specific with which to work. Use it as is until you've had enough experience to understand the more advanced subtleties of the game.

When you send your dog on a blind retrieve, in training or in hunting, you will maintain excellent control if you keep him within a fairway thusly defined. In dog-games, you may need to shrink the fairway somewhat. The 20 percent rule will get you by under most hunt test judges—but not all, so be observant. Study how the pros and experienced amateurs define the fairway for each blind. Ask them, or better yet, observe how much leeway they allow their dogs before blowing the whistle. In time, this will hone your fairway concept more precisely. Because field trials are competitive, their fairways have become narrower and narrower over the years, until they are now downright anorectic. Watching field trial handlers keep their dogs on a tightrope through hell-and-high-water all the way to a 300-plus yard blind makes a person recall what golfer, Sam Snead, once said about a certain golf course: "Why, those fairways are so narrow we had to walk down them single file!"

LINE MANNERS

During my early years in retrievers, experienced people told me that, to set a dog up for a blind retrieve, the handler absolutely had to align his spine properly. "He'll run in the direction his spine indicates, so line his spine up right and he'll take a good line." Over the years, I've found that to be more than a little misleading. Granted, proper spine alignment helps, but *the critical factor, the one that overrides all else, is proper alignment of his head, and more specifically his eyes.* The dog will run the way he's looking, whether his spine is aligned that way or not. Remember, he will run to his "picture," the one he's staring at as he sits at the line. If his spine is also aimed that way, so much the better, but his head and eyes will trump all else.

To get a good line from your dog, you should help him focus on a good picture. *As soon as he is solidly focused on the picture you want, send him!* Any hesitation from you at that point will only worsen his picture, and hence his initial line. Okay, with that thought in mind, let's go back through the steps you should take in setting your dog up at the line for a blind retrieve.

When you arrive at the line, point your left foot (the one nearest your dog) toward the bird. If you use this foot as a reference, you won't have to glance back and forth between your dog's head and the bird time after time after time. Now, get your dog to sit at heel beside you with his spine aligned as close to the line to the bird as possible. Tell him that this is a blind retrieve. (I use the cue *Dead bird!* for this.) Watch his head. When he locks in on a picture, determine from your left foot whether his picture is reasonably good. If so, you should confirm it with your left hand and the cue *Good!* (I used *Line!* for many years, until I heard field trialer Roger Fuller use *Good!* That makes so much sense, for the dog already knows what it means, whereas you must teach him what *Line!* means.) Then you should send him, which most retrieverites do with *Back!* Thus your blind retrieve sequence is *Dead bird!—Good!— Back!* First you give the cue-word *Dead bird!* to tell your dog he is about to run a blind retrieve rather than a mark. Second you give another cue-word, *Good!*, to tell him he has a reasonable picture. Finally you send him on his way with the command-word *Back!*

When you confirm your dog's picture with *Good!*, you should also put your left hand alongside his head as an added cue. Today, most handlers put the hand directly over the center of the dog's head. That's okay—as long as it doesn't block the dog's view of his picture. However, in judging, I've seen many an overwrought handler shove his mitt down in front of his dog's muzzle, thereby totally blocking his vision of *anything!* That's why I recommend placing your hand *alongside* your dog's head, where he can see it out of the corner of his eye, but where it can't block his vision, no matter how up-tight you happen to be at the moment. (*See* photo on page 16.) Take your choice, but remember that, wherever you put your left hand, you are simply confirming a picture he already has. You shouldn't wave it around trying to give him a different picture. Those who, in dog-games, block their dog's vision are usually trying to do precisely that—and in the process make any picture, good or bad, impossible.

Another important point about your left hand: Don't move it as you send your dog. If you do, it will distract him from his picture—at the worst possible instant.

But what if, after you set him up, he has the wrong picture? Since you use your left hand only to confirm a good picture, you shouldn't put it down there when he has a bad one—nor should you say *Good!*, since that, too, is used only to confirm a good picture. Instead, say *No*. Then do whatever it takes to help him find a better picture: To pull his head toward you, pat your left leg; to push his head away from you, bend your right knee and move it toward him. (Here I'm assuming he is sitting on your left side.) If those techniques don't work, re-heel him. Shift around a little, commanding *Heel!* as you do. In extreme cases, heel him around in a small circle and start over. In short, do whatever you have to do to help him find a good picture before you go any further with this particular blind retrieve.

Perhaps I should emphasize that as soon as he has a good picture, you should confirm it (left hand and *Good!*), and then send him (*Back!*)—*quickly*. In judging, I've watched so many handlers turn what would have been a great blind into a mediocrity by not sending their dogs when they were ready to go. The dog quickly goes slack, then changes or loses his picture. Often this creates panic in the handler, who hollers a foolish *Back!* The dog takes a "P.I.L." (poor initial line), forcing the handler to blow his whistle almost immediately. Frustrated, the handler forgets his normal handling rhythm and flails his arms about wildly. The dog becomes bewildered. Often the result is a hack-job all the way to the bird. To avoid this, send your dog immediately after you confirm (with *Good!*) that he has a good picture. If his picture isn't good enough to justify sending him immediately, don't confirm it!

"SHOPPING" IN DUMMY PILE

In most lining drills, you send your dog to a "dummy pile," that is, several dummies in a slightly scattered group. This allows you to run the drill several times without having to walk out and put down a fresh dummy each time. Most dogs will, at least at first, react to this assortment of treasures like a kid trying to pick just one flavor from the assortment in an ice cream parlor. The dog will pick up a dummy, drop it, pick up another, and so on, before bringing one in. Most dogs gradually overcome this little failing, which we call "shopping," for obvious reasons.

Some trainers, especially pros training many dogs, have zero tolerance for such pottering around. So before beginning lining drills with a new dog, most pros take the animal through a little backyard drill to cure him of shopping. The trainer spreads a few dummies on the ground, straps the e-collar on the dog, and then heels him toward and through the dummy pile. As he goes through it, he commands *Fetch!* If the dog is the least bit indecisive about which dummy he wants, the trainer zaps him with the e-collar until he has one in his mouth. Back and forth they go this way. Eventually, the dog loses all curiosity about which is the "perfect" dummy, and just grabs one.

Next, the trainer heels the dog to a spot near the dummy pile. He stops and the dog sits beside him. Pointing at the dummy pile, he commands *Fetch!* If the dog shops, or even hesitates over the pile, the trainer zaps him until he has a dummy in his mouth. After a few sessions of this, the dog no longer shops.

There are a zillion additional drills of this type, and some people take their dogs through an unbelievable number of them, apparently not realizing they all serve the same purpose. If your blood boils while watching your dog shop in the dummy pile, you should cure him with this simple little drill, and then get on with your training. You don't have to take him through a maze of similar drills.

4
Lining Drills for Land

Of the three parts of a blind retrieve, lining is the most difficult to teach, the most difficult to maintain, and therefore, the one to which trainers devote most of their drilling time. In real blind retrieves, the dog must run long, straight lines to birds he hasn't seen fall. Before a dog will do this, such lining must have become a conditioned response for him. Conditioning requires drilling, in this case drills in which the dog runs long, straight lines to unseen but known dummy piles.

Over the years trainers have developed many such drills. Like all human inventions, these have been a mixed bag. In general, those that encourage the dog to use "pictures" are the most effective, especially during the initial phases of training. Of the drills described in this chapter, the following drills encourage pictures: visual aid pattern blinds, modern sight blinds, classical sight blinds, permanent pattern blinds, and reruns of real blinds. The following drills, which are also briefly described in this chapter, don't encourage pictures and are therefore not recommended: mowed paths, pile driving.

DRILLS

Visual Aid Pattern Blind

Description
    In this trial-and-success drill, the trainer first teaches his dog that a white visual aid (cone, flag, or whatever) marks the location of the dummy pile. Thereafter, he can set up pattern blinds anywhere, with the

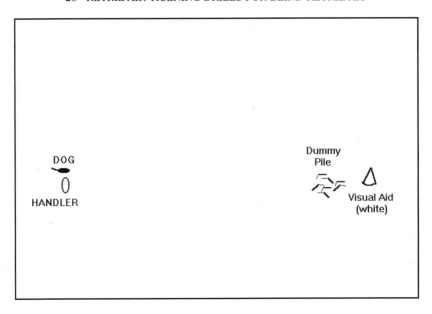

Figure 3. Visual Aid Pattern Blind.

visual aid marking the location of the dummy pile. When sent, his dog will run straight to the visual aid, and therefore to the dummies. After he does this once or twice, the trainer removes the visual aid and reruns the test without it. This "pastes pictures in the dog's album," first with and then without the visual aid.

I first learned of this technique from Margaret Patton in Tishamingo, Oklahoma, back in 1975. She said she learned it from some pro somewhere, so I have no idea where the concept originated. But whoever invented it did us all a favor. To this day, this is my favorite lining drill, my bread-and-butter pattern blind, my fall-back position for almost any lining problem.

Purpose of Drill

This drill has two basic purposes: First, it initially conditions the dog to run long and straight lines to blind retrieves; second, it facilitates introducing complexities into blind retrieves as the dog progresses. Since it can be used both on land and in water, it makes it unnecessary to switch drills between the two.

A thoroughly positive technique, it maximizes the dog's style. Since the dog always succeeds in his initial run, it helps prevent popping—that is, stopping for help without a stop-whistle—and if that fault comes up later on, the visual aid pattern blind can help overcome it.

Prerequisites

Your dog should be marking well in reasonably difficult double marked retrieves. If you start blind retrieve training too soon, you will be tempted to handle your dog on marks he can't find on his own. If you were to do this often, his marking wouldn't develop as it should.

Equipment and Facilities

You need several dummies and one visual aid, which can be any portable white object that your dog can see from the line. For years I used white traffic cones. More recently, I have switched to little white and black flags. I have heard that one person has made up "simulated cones," like tiny teepees, from three stakes and white cloth. Some people use white five-gallon paint buckets. Whatever white object you choose, when you use it in cover, you'll also need some way to elevate it for visibility. For this I use wooden stakes.

Initially, when you are moving back to lengthen your dog's lines in each successive run, you should wear a training or hunting vest with a gamebag in which you can carry the dummies he delivers to you. That way, you won't accidentally drop delivered dummies on the ground, where they would interfere with your dog's next run.

Initially you need a flat field at least 85 by 30 yards, with light cover and a lengthwise wind (so you can run your dog with the wind). Later on, you will need various fields in which to set up these pattern blinds so your dog must go through hazards.

Precautions and Pitfalls

It has often been alleged that these visual aids encourage dogs to run to any white objects that may be lying around, such as white plastic cups and bottles, loose pieces of paper, or even decoys with lots of white coloring. In one sense, that is a foolish accusation, in that all dogs tend to do that anyhow. If you doubt that, just see what a handler does when something white (paper plate, plastic cup, or whatever) blows into the middle of a test just before he comes to the line. He will ask the judges to have it removed, because its presence creates an unfair situation, one the other dogs have not had to deal with.

But, in another sense, this accusation may seem to have merit. Teaching a dog to run to certain white objects will definitely exacerbate his natural inclination to run to *any* white object. However, as you will see in Chapter 10, you can more easily cure your dog of running to random white objects if you first teach him to run to white visual aids. Thus, the very visual aids that intensify the problem also facilitate the cure. In dog training, "it doesn't get any better than that!"

When initially lengthening your dog's lines by moving back for each successive run, don't drop dummies on the ground. If you do, your dog will find them on the next longer run, which will ruin the drill. Even if you pick dropped dummies up, the scent will remain to distract him on subsequent runs. Ideally, you should wear a vest with a gamebag big enough to hold all the dummies he delivers to you.

Don't overwork your dog in any one session.

Process—Steps in Training

Start out in a flat field with light cover. Set up the visual aid at the downwind end. Grab half a dozen dummies, and heel your dog to the opposite end of the field. Now heel him from there straight toward the visual aid. When you reach a point about five yards short of the visual

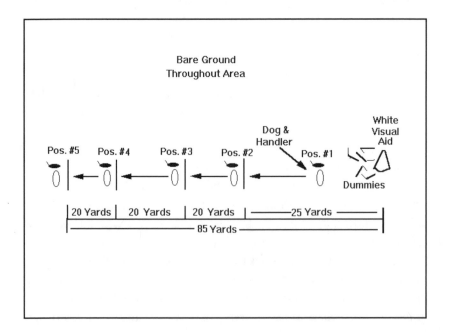

Figure 4. Introducing Visual Aid Pattern Blinds.

aid, stop and have him sit at heel beside you. Now, toss the dummies, one at a time, near the visual aid. As you toss each one, say *Dead bird!* This introduces the cue you'll always use to tell your dog he is about to run a blind retrieve.

Now heel him straight back away from the visual aid until you are about 25 yards from it. Turn to face the visual aid, with your dog sitting at heel. Go through your blind retrieve sequence (*Dead bird!—Good!—Back!*) and send him. Having just watched you toss the dummies near the visual aid, he'll run straight to the dummy pile.

As he does, you should run 15 or 20 yards in the opposite direction (to make his next run that much longer). When he returns to you with the dummy, take it (without dropping it on the ground!), and set him up to again run to the visual aid from this greater distance. Go through your blind retrieve sequence and send him.

As he goes, run back another 15 or 20 yards (again to lengthen his next run). Then, when he reaches you, repeat from there. And so on. If all goes well, within the first four or five runs, your dog will be going the full 85 yards. However, if he falters at any shorter distance, shorten up rather than lengthen his next run. Trial-and-success! Trial-and-success! A short success is better than a long failure!

Don't run him more than four or five times per session. In his second session, make his initial run about 40 yards, and lengthen him out to about 100 yards through the three or four reruns. In each subsequent session, make his initial run longer until it is whatever maximum distance you have in mind for your dog.

At some point in his first few sessions, your dog will come to understand the significance of the visual aid. When you take him out of his dog-box, he will look around for it. When he sees it, he will "lock in" (stare intently at it). When he does this, you can discontinue heeling him to the visual aid at the start of this drill. Instead, simply put the dummy pile out when you position the visual aid. With the visual aid and dummies already in place, get your dog out and heel him to your intended starting line. Face the visual aid, with your dog sitting at heel. When he locks in on it, go through your blind retrieve sequence, and send him.

After your dog understands the visual aid's place in his life's work, add complexities to his pattern blinds: terrain variations, cover variations, crosswinds. But don't run him into head winds until he is well into real blind retrieves, and seldom even then. Head winds encourage quartering, not lining.

Start removing the visual aid for his reruns. Run him once or twice with the visual aid in place to guide him. Then remove it and rerun him two or three times without it. That will help him to form pictures without the visual aid, and to run long and straight to those picture.

Addenda

Throughout your dog's active life, whenever you want to introduce him to a new blind retrieve concept—from simple hazards to highly complex mixed marks and blinds—you will progress more rapidly and with fewer human vs. canine donnybrooks if you initially use visual aids to tell your dog where the blinds are planted. Then, of course, remove the visual aids for the reruns.

As you will see in Chapter 5, you can use visual aid pattern blinds in water, too. Of course, don't attempt it until your dog is doing good work on fairly challenging visual aid pattern blinds on land.

Visual Aid Pattern Blind with an Unavoidable Hazard

Description

This is a trial-and-success extension of the above visual aid pattern blind. In this extension you use the visual aid to train your dog to carry a line through an unavoidable hazard, such as the deep ditch in the diagram. It could as well have been a creek, a car-track "road," a long patch of heavy cover, or any hazard too long for the dog to run around. In this drill, you use a visual aid to guide your dog through the hazard once or twice. Then you rerun him two or three times with the visual aid removed.

Purpose of Drill

This drill allows you to introduce your dog to hazards of this particular type. It does this in a positive way, for the visual aid tells the dog where you want him to go, thereby encouraging him to drive on through the hazard.

Prerequisites

The dog should be well advanced in his basic lining drills with visual aids. It certainly helps if your dog has had marks through similar hazards.

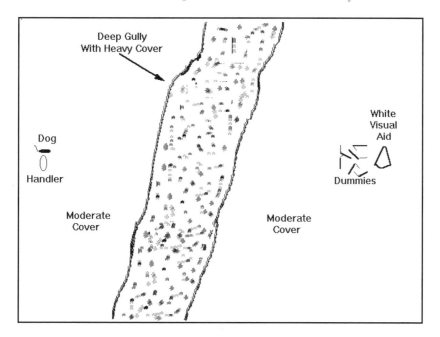

Figure 5. Visual Aid Pattern Blind with
Unavoidable Hazard.

Equipment and Facilities

You need several dummies and a visual aid. You also need a suitable location, one with this type of hazard.

Precautions and Pitfalls

Don't complicate this drill by running it through multiple hazards. Introduce your dog to one hazard at a time.

Make these pattern blinds relatively short, so you can rerun him several times.

Don't overwork your dog in any one session.

Process—Steps in Training

Set the pattern blind up according to the diagram, with the line and the visual aid on opposite sides of the hazard. To allow your dog a little running room on each side, set the test up with both the line and the visual aid at least 15 yards from the hazard.

Run your dog once or twice with the visual aid in place. If all goes well, remove it and rerun him two or three times without it.

If he spooks at the hazard—refuses to enter it, or does so with extreme caution—you should stop the drill immediately, lest you permanently traumatize him. Before trying this drill again, give him plenty of chances to become familiar with such hazards without any retrieves involved. Take him for walks in which you lead him into such hazards. While both of you are in the middle of it, stop and pet him awhile, even give him food treats. Do this in a variety of similar hazards until he loses his fear and becomes comfortable there. Then run him on marks that fall first in the middle of such hazards, then on the other side. If that works, go back to the visual aid pattern blinds.

Addenda

Most dogs pick this up quickly and easily.

Visual Aid Pattern Blind with an Avoidable Hazard

Description

This drill, which has both trial-and-success and trial-and-error phases, teaches your dog to drive straight through hazards he could easily run around—but shouldn't. For example, let's say you send your dog for a blind retrieve on the other side of a patch of heavy cover, as in the diagram. If he changes course to run around it, he'll head way off-line. Thus he'll disturb cover unnecessarily and he'll require more whistle tooting and arm waving from you than he should.

You begin this drill in a "friendly" trial-and-success way by setting the line up right in the middle of the hazard, where your dog can't avoid it. Then you move the line back a little further for each successive rerun. Eventually, your dog will try an end run around the hazard. When he does, you go into trial-and-error mode, correcting him with the e-collar.

This drill is the blind retrieve equivalent of the drill in the companion volume, *Retriever Training Drills for Marking*, for teaching straight lines through hazards on marks.

Purpose of Drill

This drill teaches the dog to carry the line given him even when it takes him through an avoidable hazard.

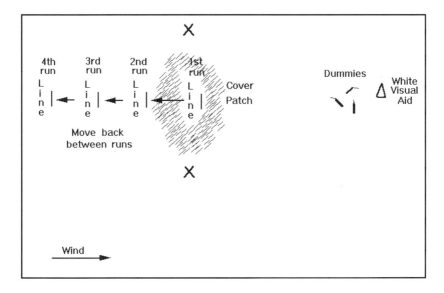

Figure 6. Visual Aid Pattern Blind
with Avoidable Hazard.

Prerequisites

The dog should be well along in his initial lining drills with visual aids, including taking lines through unavoidable hazards. He should also have been taught to go through avoidable hazards on marks.

He should have been e-collar-conditioned.

Equipment and Facilities

You need several dummies and a visual aid. You need an e-collar, preferably with momentary stimulation.

You need a suitable location, one with such a hazard.

Precautions and Pitfalls

To make sure the dog can distinguish between the correct line and the route around, you should do this drill with a fairly wide hazard, one about 40 yards wide. That way, when you nick him for running around the hazard, regardless of which side he takes, he will be 20 yards from the true line. If you were to nick him for running around a narrow patch, he would be so close to where he should be that he would almost surely misunderstand the correction. That leads inevitably to no-go's.

Don't overwork your dog in any one session.

Process—Steps in Training

Set the pattern blind up according to the diagram, with the blind at least 40 yards downwind of the patch of cover. Set your dog up in the middle of the cover and send him from there, where he cannot avoid the cover. This "patterns" him to run through the hazard.

Next, run him from immediately behind the cover patch. Here again, he really can't avoid the hazard. This run, too, patterns him.

Next, move back perhaps 15 or 20 yards. Because of the previous patterning runs, he will probably go through the cover again. But he may avoid it on the way back. That would be great good fortune, for it allows you to correct him on his return rather than on his way out. Corrections on the return can't induce no-go's. So, if he avoids the cover on the return, nick him with the e-collar when he reaches either of the indicated spots (X) in the diagram.

With this correction, you are creating a hot-spot outside the cover. That's why you nick him at the widest point in his end run. Were you to nick him anywhere else on his route around the hazard, you would risk turning the cover into a hot-spot.

If you corrected him on the return, rerun him from the same line. He will probably drive through the hazard going out, but may do any of three things on his return. He may again come around the cover on the same side, but this time swinging much wider. If he does, again nick him at the widest point of his end run. He may run around the hazard on the opposite side. If he does, nick him at the spot marked with an "X" in the diagram. Or, happily, he may return straight through the hazard. Continue to rerun him (assuming he's not too tired) from the same line until he does indeed return straight through.

Then, move back another 15 or 20 yards and run him again. If all goes well, move back again and run him again (always assuming he's not too tired). And so on, until he finally runs around the cover going out, which he will do sooner or later (and probably sooner). When he does, nick him with the e-collar at the place indicated on the diagram. Say nothing. Let him continue on and complete the retrieve. Rerun him for the same line. If he runs around the cover on the opposite side, nick him there. If he goes straight through going and returning, congratulate yourself! You've begun to convince him that the "bumblebees" swarm only outside the hazard.

If he's still fresh, remove the visual aid and rerun him a couple of times without it. This will cement the lesson in his mind better.

Addenda

If your dog has already done this drill on marks, he should have little difficulty with it here.

Modern Sight Blind

Description

Over the years, two trial-and-success drills have been called "sight blind." To distinguish between them, I've called the older one "classical" and the newer one "modern." Since the latter is more useful, I'm describing it first.

In the modern sight blind, the trainer puts out the dummy pile and has an assistant hide somewhere near it. After bringing his dog to the line, the trainer signals for his assistant to "mark the pile." The assistant steps out into plain sight and tosses a dummy so it lands in the dummy

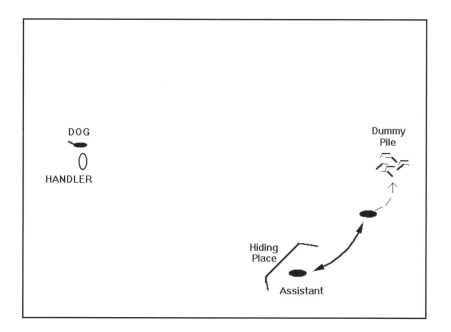

Figure 7. Modern Sight Blind.

pile. The dog sees this, so he now knows where the pile is. The assistant returns to his hiding place. Then the trainer lines his dog to the pile, and gives him an appropriate number of reruns. The first run is little more than a marked retrieve, but the reruns are true sight blinds, in that the dog runs to a "picture."

Purpose of Drill

Like the visual aid pattern blind, this is an introductory drill for lining. You can use either one, or both, when first training your dog to line.

Like the visual aid pattern blind, this drill allows you to set up pattern blinds anywhere. Your dog will line every one on his first run. Thus, it teaches long and straight lines and discourages popping. Also, like the visual aid pattern blind, you can use this drill throughout your dog's active life to introduce hazards and various blind retrieve concepts.

Prerequisites

Your dog should be marking well in reasonably difficult double marked retrieves. If you start blind retrieve training too soon, you will be tempted to handle your dog on marks he can't find on his own. If you were to do this often, his marking would never develop as it should.

Equipment and Facilities

You need an assistant with several dummies. Initially, you need a flat field at least 85 by 30 yards, with light cover, a place in which your assistant can hide, and a lengthwise wind (so you can run your dog with the wind). Later on, you will need fields with a variety of hazards.

Precautions and Pitfalls

Because your dog sees your assistant near the dummy pile, this drill exacerbates the dog's natural inclination to suck back to marks in tests having both marks and blinds. However, since you must cure that problem anyhow, this slight increase in his natural tendency shouldn't deter you from using the modern sight blind. However, if your assistant were to remain visible throughout the drill, that would make curing the suction problem immeasurably more difficult. So keep your assistant out of sight except when he marks the pile.

Don't overwork your dog in any one session.

Process—Steps in Training

Start with a short test, no more than 50 yards, in light cover on fairly flat land. Set it up so your dog runs with the wind going to the dummy pile. Put out the dummy pile and have your assistant hide nearby.

Bring your dog to the line and set him up there. Signal for your assistant to mark the pile. He should step out into plain sight and toss a dummy so it lands in the dummy pile. Then he should return to his hiding place.

Go through your blind retrieve sequence and send your dog. He will race directly to the pile. Rerun him two or three times (without your assistant marking the pile). Then put him up.

In subsequent sessions, gradually lengthen the tests out to whatever maximum distance you plan to use. Then add terrain and cover hazards as described above in the drills with visual aids. In each test, have your assistant mark the pile for only the initial run, never for the reruns.

Addenda

This drill has the same range of uses as the visual aid pattern blind, except that it requires an assistant. The visual aid pattern blind slightly exacerbates a dog's natural inclination to go to loose white objects. This drill slightly exacerbates his natural inclination to suck back to marks in mixed tests. Since you have to cure both problems anyhow, no serious argument can be made against either drill.

Classical Sight Blind

Description

This trial-and-success drill is the parent of both the visual aid pattern blind and the modern sight blind. I first read about it in Paul Shoemaker's out-of-print 1970 book, *Training Retrievers for Field Trials and Hunting*. It was the first lining drill I encountered that actually encouraged the dog to use pictures. Thus it has historical significance, even though trainers have abandoned it in favor of its two more productive offspring.

In this drill, the trainer first selects the locations for both the line and the blind, but puts out no dummy pile. He grabs a few dummies and carries them as he heels his dog from the line to the intended location

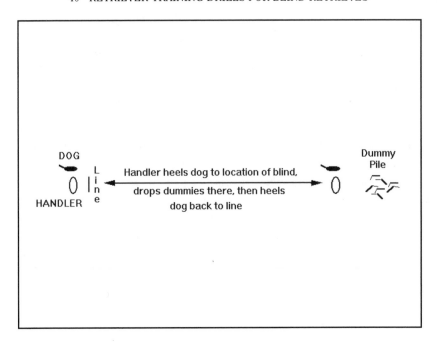

DOG

HANDLER

Line

Handler heels dog to location of blind, drops dummies there, then heels dog back to line

Dummy Pile

Figure 8. Classical Sight Blind.

of the dummy pile. There, with his dog sitting at heel and watching, he tosses the dummies to the intended spot. Then he heels him back to the line, sets him up, and sends him. The dog will run straight to the dummies he just watched the trainer put out. Then the trainer reruns his dog two or three times.

Purpose of Drill

This is another introductory drill, intended for the dog just learning to line. With enough repetitions in enough locations, it conditions the dog to run long straight lines to blind retrieves. It discourages popping, because the dog always finds the dummies without being handled to them. It encourages the dog to focus on a picture at the line, because he knows where the dummies are.

Prerequisites

Your dog should be marking well in reasonably difficult double marked retrieves. If you start blind retrieve training too soon, you will be tempted to handle your dog on marks he can't find on his own. If you were to do this often, his marking would never develop as it should.

Equipment and Facilities

You need a few dummies and a suitable location. Initially, you need only a flat field at least 85 by 30 yards, with light cover and a lengthwise wind (so you can run your dog downwind). Later you will need fields with various hazards.

Precautions and Pitfalls

This drill takes a lot of time, because you must heel the dog all the way to and from the location of the blind before you run him the first time. If you are training more than one dog, this becomes a serious problem.

This drill can be used only on land, so you'll need another lining drill for water.

Don't overwork your dog in any one session.

Process—Steps in Training

Start out on fairly level ground with light cover, and set the drill up so your dog will be running downwind. Start short, say, with 50-yard retrieves, so your dog will find the dummies quickly and easily.

Select a specific spot for the blind and another specific spot for the line. Grab several dummies, and slip a lead on your dog. Heel him first to the line. Stop there with him sitting at heel facing the location of the blind. Now, heel him straight toward the blind. When you are within a few feet of it, stop and have him sit at heel. Toss the dummies, one at a time, to the intended spot, saying *Dead bird!* with each toss (to accustom him to this cue). Heel him directly back to the line and turn around to face the blind, with your dog sitting at heel. Go through your blind retrieve sequence (*Dead bird!—Good!—Back!*). Because he saw you put the dummies out, he'll run straight to them. Rerun him two or three times.

In subsequent sessions, make these sight blinds longer and more complex (involving different hazards).

Addenda

Frankly, as far as I know, no one still uses the classical sight blind. Trainers prefer its two offspring, the visual aid pattern blind and the modern sight blind—and for good reasons. In fact, I no longer recommend the classical sight blind. But I had to include it because of its historic significance. As far as I know, it was the first lining drill that encouraged the dog to use pictures.

Permanent Pattern Blind

Trainers with permanent training grounds often set up a number of pattern blinds as permanent fixtures, some on land, some in water, some involving both. Each blind has a different type of hazard, or a different set of hazards. These trainers—pros or fortunate amateurs—introduce each new dog to various hazards with these permanent pattern blinds. They also "refresh" older dogs on various concepts this way.

To take full advantage of permanent pattern blinds, you need marvelous training grounds. Granted, many trainers not blessed with such grounds have permanent pattern blinds established here and there. But to maximize the benefits of such drills, you need, as an old song said, "Land, lots of land, under starry skies above," and that land had better have plenty of suitable water, too! If you are so blessed, study your grounds and design a set of permanent blinds that will maximize the benefits you can gain from the hazards you have available. If you are an inexperienced amateur, have a pro or experienced amateur help you plan them.

First, teach your dog each permanent blind as a visual aid pattern blind, a modern sight blind, or even a classical sight blind. Then, after the dog is familiar with the blind itself, discontinue these introductory techniques. Simply run the blind as is.

Real Blind Reruns

Whenever you rerun your dog on anything, you are drilling him. Thus, after he completes a real blind retrieve in training, if you immediately rerun it, as you normally should, you are drilling. This is an excellent drill, too, for your dog now knows where the dummy pile is. He will take a better line on the rerun, and he will run with greater confidence. The rerun partially offsets any hacking you may have had to do to get him to the dummy pile on his initial run.

In recent years, a few prominent field trial pros have been evangelizing against rerunning blind retrieves. They argue that it encourages the dog to suck back to old blinds in multiple blind retrieve tests. Since all dogs have a natural inclination to suck back that way, you must cure it before you can run your dog on multiple blinds. Rerunning blinds may slightly increase that tendency, and thereby make the cure somewhat more difficult. However, the benefits of rerunning blinds far outweigh this slight disadvantage, at least for hunters and hunt testers. I will grant that some field trial double blinds are so "snug" that sucking back becomes a major problem. So, if you're a field trialer, perhaps you shouldn't rerun blind retrieves. However, if you're a hunter or hunt tester, you should.

Mowed Path Pattern Blind

The late Richard Wolters' 1964 book, *Water Dog*, first documented this technique and it became very popular, at least for a time. I haven't seen it used, or even mentioned, for years. This is partially because of its own weaknesses and partially because better techniques have come out. Even so, it has at least some historical significance, so I'm including a little about it here.

In this approach, you mow long paths (typically 100 to 300 yards) through the cover. Then you put the dummy pile at one end and teach your dog to run lines by staying in the mowed path. As in the visual aid pattern blind, you start short and lengthen out fairly quickly, after which you run only the full length.

This technique has several weaknesses. Perhaps the greatest is that it teaches a dog to run down any path he may find—car tracks, or even cow trails. Field trial judges figured this out very quickly, and began running blind retrieves that angled across some sort of path. Dogs trained on mowed paths didn't do so well in such tests. Another weakness is that mowed paths don't encourage the dog to use pictures. And, of course, you can't use them in water. Finally, to keep your mowed paths mowed, you have to spend too much of your training time pushing a lawn mower.

Pile Driving

This trial-and-error introductory technique is usually called "driving to a pile," but I prefer the more graphic expression, "pile driving."

Simply stated, it extends force-breaking into a lining drill. It has produced many of our top field trial dogs, so it has undeniable merit.

However, it is a totally negative approach. The trainer literally drives the dog to the dummy pile, hastening his steps first with the whip, then with marbles from a slingshot, and finally with electricity from the e-collar. These forms of "pressure" (= punishment) do indeed induce the dog to move rapidly, which passes for style, at least among those who can't distinguish between speed and style.

Field trialers must get very fine lines from their dogs, and pile driving certainly accomplishes that. So, if you are a field trialer, by all means, learn this technique, which you can do by visiting almost any pro. Better yet, have the pro do it for you. But, if you are not a field trialer, you shouldn't play monkey-see-monkey-do with this technique. You can get good enough lines for your purposes with the other, more gentle, lining techniques recommended in this book. Enough said.

5
Lining Drills for Water

In actual hunting, most blind retrieves occur in waterfowling, and therefore in water. In dog-games, the most challenging blinds are in water. So, not surprisingly, trainers devote a significant portion of their time working on blind retrieves in water, or "water blinds," as they are more commonly called. Small wonder then that some over-eager beginners jump into this phase of training before their dogs are ready for it. Unfortunately, the slowest, most uncertain way to approach the water blind is to rush into it. Dogs are land, not water, mammals. If they were water mammals, they'd have gills and fins! Being genetic landlubbers, they learn most easily and most quickly on *terra firma*. As a matter of fact, we *teach* them absolutely nothing in water. We do all the teaching on land—and then extend that canine erudition into water. This sequence is necessary in marks, which is in the genes. Clearly, it's even more so in blind retrieves, which are totally taught. Thus, you should first teach your retriever each of the three parts of the blind retrieve on land, and extend them into water only after he has mastered them on land. If you push him into water work too rapidly, he will almost certainly balk, forcing you go back to land and bring him forward again. The more often you repeat this mistake, the longer it will take you to teach him water blinds. *Verba sapientibus.*

This chapter contains eight lining drills for water. Three (visual aid pattern blind, modern sight blind, and permanent blind) are water adaptations of similar lining drills for land covered in Chapter 4. Of the other five, one (floating white dummy blind) is an extremely basic introductory drill. The other four (angled entry drill, angled exit drill, points and islands drill, and channel blind drill) are advanced drills to deal with "water cheating." A retriever "cheats the water" when he detours by land instead of carrying the line given him through the water.

DRILLS

Floating White Dummy Blind

Description

This extremely basic trial-and-success drill teaches the dog to enter water on command even though he has not actually seen a fall. In it, the trainer lines his dog to a highly visible big white dummy floating in calm water. Before bringing him to the line, the trainer tosses the dummy out into the water wherever he wants it. Thus, the dog doesn't actually see a fall. However, when set up at the line, he sees the white dummy floating there. When sent, he'll jump in and retrieve it.

Purpose of Drill

If you like "groaner" puns, you could call this drill an "ice-breaker for cold water blinds." (A "cold" blind retrieve is one that's run all by

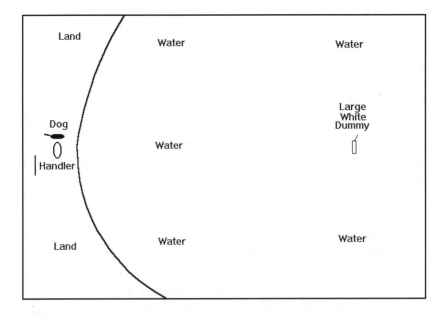

Figure 9. Floating White Dummy Blind.

itself, not as part of a "mixed" test having both marks and blinds.) This drill induces the dog to enter water on command when he has not seen a fall. It builds confidence in both the dog and in the beginning trainer (who at first may have doubts about his ability to teach his dog water blinds).

Prerequisites

The dog should be well along in his basic lining drills on land before starting any type of water lining drill.

Equipment and Facilities

You need one big white dummy, or if you opt for the rerun technique involving a string of dummies in a straight line (see below), you need several big white dummies.

You need a pond or lake with calm water.

Precautions and Pitfalls

Before you bring your dog to the line, squat down and check to see whether the dummy is adequately visible from his level.

Don't do this drill in choppy water. Even if your dog can see the dummy from the line, he won't be able to see it as he swims. It will drift away and won't be where he expects it to be. So, he may give up and return to you, which would be a disaster. Or, he may find the dummy after swimming around this way and that as the dummy plays hide-and-seek with him, which wouldn't be much better. When you send him on a line, you want him to go straight and find the dummy while doing so, especially at this early stage of training.

Don't overwork your dog in any one session.

Process—Steps in Training

Leaving your dog someplace where he can't watch, go to the shoreline and toss a big white dummy out 20 or 25 yards into calm water. Then bring your dog to the line. When he locks in on the dummy, go through your blind retrieve sequence and send him.

If you want to rerun him, you'll have to put him up again while you toss the dummy out for the rerun. That being the case, you may as well move to another spot on the pond and start over.

Optionally, to facilitate reruns as well as to lengthen your dog out a little with this drill, you can start out by tossing out a series of white dummies in a straight line, say every five yards from 25 to 50 yards from the line. Then have your dog pick them up one at a time, always picking up the nearest one, of course.

Addenda

Don't waste too much time with this drill. One or two sessions should be enough to accustom him to entering water on command without seeing a fall. Then move on to other drills.

Visual Aid Pattern Blind

Description

This is the water version of the trial-and-success visual aid pattern blind drill for land described in Chapter 4.

Purpose of Drill

This drill introduces the "green" retriever to water blinds with no risk of failure. It can also be used to add complexities to the water blinds of more experienced dogs.

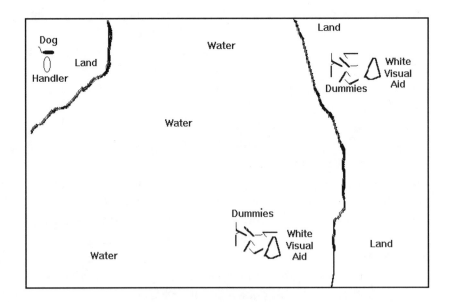

Figure 10. Two Setups for Visual Aid
Pattern Blinds in Water.

Prerequisites

The dog should understand the significance of the visual aid, and should be well along in his lining drills on land. Although not absolutely necessary, running a few floating dummy drills (above) first does indeed better prepare the dog for this drill.

Equipment and Facilities

You need a white visual aid (flag, cone, plastic bottle, box, or whatever), several dummies, and a suitable pond or lake.

Precautions and Pitfalls

Don't add complexities too rapidly. In other words, use the K.I.S.S. approach (Keep It Simple, Stupid!). For example, until your dog is well advanced in this drill, set it up so he won't be tempted to detour by land. Give him a square (90-degree) entry into the water and a square exit from the water, with no points or islands near his path from the line and the visual aid.

Don't overwork your dog in any one session.

Process—Steps in Training

As the diagram shows, you can set the dummy pile up in either of two ways: on land across water, or in the water itself. Whenever you opt for the latter, you must prop the visual aid up above the surface somehow. For this, I've always used wooden stakes stuck in the bottom of the lake.

You should put the dummy pile actually in the water as often as you can. That prevents your dog from thinking that water blinds are always on land on the other side of the water. Such thinking encourages water cheating. After all, why should the dog get wet if the dummy pile is always somewhere on land? Unfortunately, circumstances will often prevent you from putting the dummies out in the water. The water may be too deep for you to wade out to set up your visual aid. Or, as happens quite often, a strong or gusty wind would scatter floating dummies all over the lake. However, you should put the dummy pile out in the water whenever you can.

With the visual aid and dummy pile in place, bring your dog to the line. When he locks in on the visual aid, go through your blind retrieve sequence and send him. He'll jump in and swim straight to the visual aid.

Then, remove the visual aid and rerun him a couple of times without it. That helps him form water blind pictures both with and without the visual aid.

As on land, gradually make these pattern blinds longer and more complex.

Addenda

You should use either this drill or the modern sight blind (below) for the trial-and-success phase of every new water blind concept you teach your dog.

Modern Sight Blind

Description

This is the water version of the trial-and-success modern sight blind for land described in Chapter 4.

Purpose of Drill

Like the visual aid pattern blind, you can use this drill to introduce the "green" retriever to basic water blinds and to introduce the more advanced dog to more challenging water blind concepts.

Prerequisites

Your dog should be well along in his lining drills on land. Although not absolutely necessary, running a few floating dummy drills (above) first does indeed better prepare the dog for this drill.

Equipment and Facilities

You need an assistant, some dummies, and a suitable pond or lake. You need a place, near the dummy pile, where your assistant can hide before and after he "marks" the pile.

Precautions and Pitfalls

Your assistant should stay hidden except when actually marking the pile. If he remains visible, your dog will form an extremely strong habit of sucking back to marks in mixed tests.

Don't add complexities too rapidly. In other words, use the K.I.S.S. approach (Keep It Simple, Stupid!). For example, until your dog is well advanced in this drill, set it up so he won't be tempted to detour by land. Give him a square (90-degree) entry into the water and a square exit from the water, with no points or islands near his path from the line and the dummy pile.

Don't overwork your dog in any one session.

Process—Steps in Training

Put out your dummy pile either in the water or on land across the water. The former is to be preferred whenever possible. About the only situation in which you cannot put the dummies in the water is when the wind will scatter them.

Have your assistant hide somewhere near the dummy pile. Bring your dog to the line and signal for your assistant to mark the pile. He should step out into plain sight, toss a dummy into the pile, and then return to his hiding place. Go through your blind retrieve sequence and send your dog. Then rerun him a time or two without having your assistant mark the pile.

Gradually add length and complexities to this drill.

Addenda

You should use either this drill or the visual aid pattern blind (above) for the trial-and-success phase of every new water blind concept you teach your dog.

Angled Entry Drill

Description

This mostly trial-and-error drill is the blind retrieve version of the angle-in drill for marks described in the companion book, *Retriever Training Drills for Marking*.

In a preliminary trial-and-success phase, the trainer patterns his dog to take the angle into the water. First he tosses a mark into the water on the line to the blind, so that the dog takes the correct angle into the water. Then he sets up either a visual aid pattern blind or modern sight blind with the same angled entry. Only after the dog takes the angle in these preliminary steps does the trainer advance him into the trial-and-error phase.

In trial-and-error mode, the trainer leaves the dummy pile where

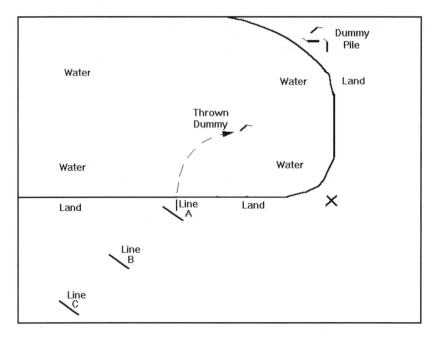

Figure 11. Angled Entry Drill.

it was for the patterning blind, but he removes the visual aid or the assistant who has been marking the pile. Then, in successive runs to the known dummy pile, the trainer moves the line back farther each time. Eventually, the dog will run around the shoreline instead of swimming. When he does, the trainer nicks him with the e-collar when he reaches the corner. Then, before rerunning him from the same spot, he repeats the mark in the water. And so on.

Purpose of Drill

This drill uses the e-collar's hot-spotting capabilities to teach the dog to take angles into water in blind retrieves, even when he sees an inviting path on land that leads to the dummy pile.

Prerequisites

The dog should be well along in his water lining drills before doing this one. He should also have been cured of running the bank on marks. (See the companion book, *Retriever Training Drills for Marking*.) And he should have been e-collar-conditioned.

Equipment and Facilities

You need several dummies and an e-collar, preferably with mometary stimulation. You need either a visual aid or an assistant to mark the pile.

You need a suitable pond, one with the angled entry and square exit this drill requires.

Precautions and Pitfalls

If you have an assistant mark the pile, make sure he stays hidden except when actually marking the pile. If he remains visible, your dog will form an extremely strong habit of sucking back to marks in mixed tests.

Remember to "re-pattern" your dog with the mark after each e-collar correction.

To allow for adequate reruns, keep the swimming distance as short as possible. You're teaching your dog angled entries, Old Thing, not preparing him to swim the English Channel!

Don't overwork your dog in any one session.

Process—Steps in Training

Set this drill up according to the diagram. Bring your dog to line A, near shore, and toss a dummy into the water so it falls on the line to the blind. Send your dog for it as a mark. This preconditions him to take the angle into the water, for he can't get to the dummy without getting wet.

Next run the blind. Initially, either use a visual aid or have an assistant mark the pile, but discontinue this after your dog succeeds once.

On his first run, with either the visual aid or marked pile, your dog will probably take the angle in and go to the dummy pile. However, if you're lucky, he'll run the bank coming back. If he does, nick him with the e-collar as he comes around the bend (at the spot marked with an "X" in the diagram), but say nothing.

Back up to line B and rerun the blind (again without the visual aid, without having the dummy pile marked). If he takes the angle, wonderful! If not, nick him with the e-collar as he rounds the bend, but say nothing. Let him continue to the dummy pile. If he returns by land, nick him again.

If your dog ran the bank, remain at line B, and re-pattern him to go by water. To do this, again toss a dummy so it falls in the water on the line to the blind and send your dog for it as a mark. Then repeat the blind—and the corrections if necessary.

When he takes the angle from line B, move back to line C and repeat the process.

Addenda

To thoroughly condition your dog to take angles into the water, you will have to do this drill many times in many places. Then, to keep him sharp on angles, you'll have to refresh his memory fairly often.

Angled Exit Drill

Description

This trial-and-error drill is the blind retrieve version of the angle-out drill for marks described in the companion book, *Retriever Training Drills for Marking*.

In a preliminary trial-and-success phase, the trainer patterns his dog by tossing a dummy into the water but near the dummy pile on the

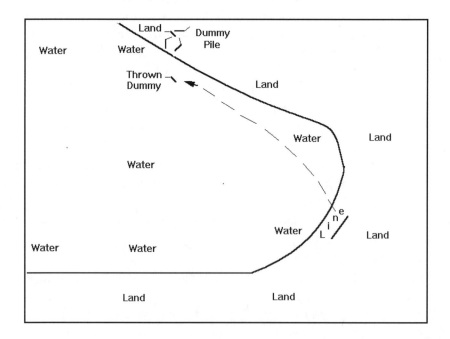

Figure 12. Angled Exit Drill.

far shore. He sends his dog for the tossed dummy as a mark. Then he runs his dog on the blind to the dummy pile, first with and then without either a visual aid or a marked dummy pile. At some point on his way to the dummy pile, the dog will almost certainly cheat. He'll cut into shore before he should rather than carry the angle to the exit point near the dummy pile. When he does, the trainer nicks him with the e-collar.

Purpose of Drill

This drill uses the e-collar's hot-spotting capabilities to teach the dog to carry angles when exiting from water rather than to veer into shore at the first convenient spot.

Prerequisites

The dog should have been taught to take angled entries with the above drill. He should also have gone through the related angle-out drill for marks. (See the companion book, *Retriever Training Drills for Marking*). He should have been e-collar-conditioned.

Equipment and Facilities

You need several dummies. You need either a visual aid or an assistant to mark the pile. You need an e-collar, preferably with momentary stimulation.

You need a suitable pond, one that allows you to set this test up with a square entry near the line and an angled exit near the dummy pile.

Precautions and Pitfalls

Don't be excessively picky about his exit point. If you nick him too near the dummy pile, he won't understand what he is doing wrong. To avoid such confusion, give him a little leeway from the true line. Ideally, the exit point should be square with a long angled shoreline going away from it. However, places like that are hard to find. Most of us have to make do with the ponds we have available to us.

If you have an assistant mark the pile, make sure he stays hidden except when actually marking the pile. If he remains visible, your dog will form an extremely strong habit of sucking back to marks in mixed tests.

Don't forget to re-pattern your dog with the mark after each e-collar correction.

Since this drill requires several reruns per session, you should set it up so the swims are short.

Don't overwork your dog in any one session.

Process—Steps in Training

Set the drill up according to the diagram, with the dummy pile near shore on the far side with a long angled exit. The line should be positioned where it offers your dog a square entry.

Heel your dog to the line. Toss a dummy so it falls in the water but very near the dummy pile. Send your dog. Since the dummy is in water, he should go straight to it rather than cheating into the shore too soon.

Next, run a visual aid pattern blind or a modern sight blind to the dummy pile. Decide before you send him how much leeway you will allow him at the exit point, so you won't risk correcting him too close to the dummy pile. How much leeway he needs depends on your dog, so you must read him accurately here.

Set your dog up at the line, and run the test. If he doesn't cheat, wonderful! If he does, nick him with the e-collar immediately after he lands. Say nothing. Let him complete the retrieve. Whether or not he cheated going out, he may run the shoreline as he returns. If he does, nick him every 5 or 10 yards, beginning as soon as he is a safe distance (at least 10 yards) from the dummy pile.

If you had to correct him going out, re-pattern him with the mark tossed in the water near the dummy pile before you rerun him. Don't bother doing this if you corrected him only on the return.

Rerun him without the visual aid, without having the pile marked. If he cheats, nick him as soon as he lands. Then re-pattern him with the mark, and rerun the blind. And so on until he no longer cheats.

Addenda

This is a tough lesson for your dog to master, so you should run him on this drill in a variety of situations. Eventually, you can run it without the visual aid and without having the pile marked. When you eliminate those, you can also eliminate the initial patterning mark. However, for a long time, continue the re-patterning mark after each correction.

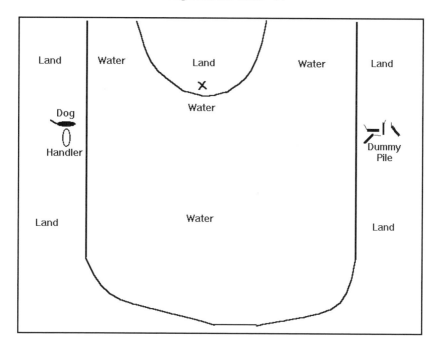

Figure 13. Points and Islands Drill.

Points and Islands Drill

Description

This trial-and-error drill is the blind retrieve version of the points and islands drill for marks described in the companion book, *Retriever Training Drills for Marking*.

First, the trainer runs his dog on either a visual aid pattern blind or a modern sight blind to a dummy pile on the far side of a body of water—with an inviting point or island somewhere near, but not on, the dog's path. If the dog cheats by veering off-course to land on the point or island, the trainer nicks him with the e-collar after he lands there. Similarly, if the dog lands on the point or island on his return trip, the trainer nicks him with the e-collar.

Then, the trainer reruns his dog to the same dummy pile, but without the visual aid, without having the pile marked. Again, if the dog lands on the point or island, going or coming, the trainer nicks him with the e-collar. Eventually, this hot-spotting technique convinces the dog to swim straight to and from the dummy pile.

Purpose of Drill

This drill uses the e-collar's hot-spotting capabilities to teach the dog to carry a line straight past inviting points and islands.

Prerequisites

The dog should be well along in his water lining drills, and should have been through the similar points and islands drill for marks. (See the companion book, *Retriever Training Drills for Marking*.) He should have been e-collar-conditioned.

Equipment and Facilities

You need several dummies and an e-collar, preferably with momentary stimulation. You need either a visual aid or an assistant to mark the pile.

You need a suitable location, a pond or lake with a point or island hazard.

Precautions and Pitfalls

If you have an assistant mark the pile, make sure he stays hidden except when actually marking the pile. If he remains visible, your dog will form an extremely strong habit of sucking back to marks in mixed tests.

Because of the point or island, the swims are necessarily longer in this drill than in the angled entry and exit drills. Thus, you should be careful not to overwork your dog in any one session.

Process—Steps in Training

Set up the test according to the diagram. To keep the line to the blind distinct from the line to the point or island, leave at least 15 yards between them at first. Keep the swim as short as possible. Initially, use either a visual aid or have an assistant mark the pile. Go through your blind retrieve sequence and send your dog. If he lands on the point or island, nick him with the e-collar but say nothing. Let him continue to the dummy pile. If he lands on the point or island coming back, nick him again but say nothing.

Rerun him. And so on. If possible, rerun him until he swims past the point or island, both going and coming, at least twice. Of course, don't overwork him to do this.

Addenda

As he learns what you want here, you can move the line to the blind a little closer to the point or island—but don't get silly about it. Keep the two lines distinct.

As in all water-cheating drills, you need to run your dog on this one in many different locations.

Channel Blind Drill

Description

This is a combination trial-and-success and trial-and-error drill that prepares a well-trained retriever for the "channel blind." That test has been a favorite of field trial judges for many decades, and it has also drifted over into hunt tests. In it, the blind is planted at one end of a long channel, and the line is set up at the other. To get through this test successfully, the dog must swim all the way, rather than landing and running down the shoreline on either side. Because the shore is so close on both sides, the temptation to cheat is doubly strong.

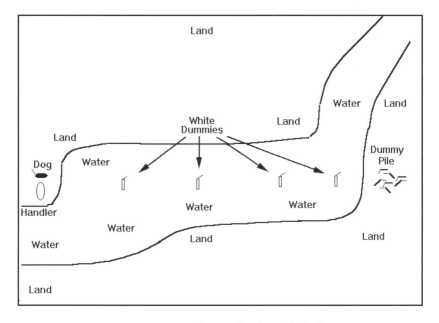

Figure 14. Introducing the Channel Blind.

Purpose of Drill

This drill uses the e-collar's hot-spotting capabilities to prepare a retriever for the infamous channel blind.

Prerequisites

The dog should be far along in all the above water-cheating drills (angled entry, angled exit, points and islands). He should have been e-collar-conditioned.

Equipment and Facilities

You need several dummies and an e-collar, preferably with momentary stimulation. You need either a visual aid or an assistant to mark the dummy pile.

You need suitable water, that is, a long, slender, fairly straight body of water, preferably with still rather than running water.

Precautions and Pitfalls

Don't start out with too long or too narrow a channel. If possible, train your dog first in one no longer than 40 yards and at least 20 yards wide. Later, after he understands this particular game, you can introduce him to longer and narrower venues.

If you have an assistant mark the pile, make sure he stays hidden except when actually marking the pile. If he remains visible, your dog will form an extremely strong habit of sucking back to marks in mixed tests.

Don't overwork your dog in any one session.

Process—Steps in Training

First the Trial-and-Success Phase: If possible, start this drill out as a string of big white dummies floating in a line down the middle of the channel, with one about every 5 to 10 yards, the last one just on shore at the far end. (This technique requires still water, of course, so the dummies don't drift.) With the dummies afloat, bring your dog to the line and set him up. When he focuses on the first dummy in the string, send him. Ditto for all the remaining dummies in the string. This will pattern him to go by water rather than by land.

Next, put out just two big white dummies, one halfway down the channel and the other one on shore at the far end. Again, he should pick them both up without incident.

Next, set up either a visual aid pattern blind or a modern sight blind in the same channel. After all the previous work, your dog should have no problem staying in the water. Rerun him a couple of times if he's not too tired.

Then the Trial-and-Error Phase: Change channels. (You'll be "channel surfing" before you finish with this drill.) Set up either a visual aid pattern blind or a modern sight blind in the new channel. This time, your dog may or may not go all the way by water. If, on the way to the dummy pile, he lands and runs the bank, nick him with the e-collar about every 5 or 10 yards from the point where he lands to about 10 yards from the dummy pile. You don't want to hot-spot the land too close to the dummy pile. If he runs the bank returning, nick him every 5 or 10 yards all the way back, but not within about 10 yards of where you are standing.

If you had to correct him going out, pattern him with a mark tossed to the middle of the channel before you rerun the blind. This mark teaches him that the water is "safe." If possible, work him in this session until he has done the entire blind correctly twice.

Thereafter, you should take him to as many different channels as you can find and repeat the above trial-and-error process.

Addenda

After you have completed all the other water-cheating drills, you should be able to get this concept through to your dog with relative ease, and relatively few corrections.

Permanent Blinds

What was said in Chapter 4 about permanent blinds on land applies equally to permanent blinds in water. If you're fortunate enough to have the facilities for them, by all means use them. Most of us don't have that much land or water that we can devote purely to retriever training, but, if you have, take advantage of what you have and set up all sorts of permanent blinds.

6
Stopping Drills

IMPORTANCE OF RELIABLE STOPPING

How important is stopping? Simply stated: *If you can't stop 'em, you can't handle 'em!* No matter how precisely your dog takes the lines you give him, and no matter how far he carries those lines, he won't line 10 percent of his blinds, especially in dog-games. Thus, in 90-plus percent of his blind retrieves, you'll have to stop him and cast him at least once (and usually more than once) to "put him on the bird," as they say.

Several years ago, while judging an AKC senior level hunting test, I watched a delightful young Chessy destroy a potentially perfect performance by refusing to stop. In the first series, a land double, he marked in typical Chesapeake fashion, which is fantastic. To ice the cake, his every move sparkled with style. In the second series, a single land blind, he took a beautiful line and carried it like a fast freight all the way to, and past, the bird. Unfortunately, he passed it only about four feet to the upwind side. Then, while his handler all but blew the sides out of his whistle trying to stop the animal, the Chessy totally ignored him. He was still hard-charging on his original line when he disappeared over a hill some 50 yards or so beyond the bird. Several minutes later he reappeared among the gallery. Heaven only knows where all he had been in the meantime. If, on his initial line, he had passed the bird so closely on the downwind side, he would have "hooked" it with his nose, and thereby lined the blind. (And, in my judging book, I would have written a big "10" followed by as many plus signs as the width of the sheet would allow!) As it was, he needed only one little "check whistle" and a soft *Over* to put him on the bird. (And, in my judging book, I would have still written a big "10," with slightly fewer plus signs.) His handler blew that check whistle—and blew it—and blew it. But the Chessy, by ignoring him, went "over the hill" and out of the hunting test.

HOW TO TOOT THE *SIT*-WHISTLE

Before you can train your retriever to respond properly and consistently to the *Sit*-whistle, you must first "train" yourself to blow it properly and consistently. (Let me hasten to add that the handler of the above-mentioned Chesapeake blew his whistle exactly as he should have. That wasn't the problem!)

The traditional whistle command to tell the dog to sit, which is normally called the *Sit*-whistle or the *Stop*-whistle, is a single sharp blast (*Tweeeeet!*). Like most traditions, this makes sense. *Tweeeeet!*, which is the simplest signal to blow, has rightly been reserved for the *Sit*-whistle, which is the retriever owner's most important whistle command. Whether you're hunting with your retriever or running him in a dog-game, the *Sit*-whistle is your court of last resort for controlling him. In upland hunting, if he ranges out too far, you use it to stop him in his tracks while you catch up, especially if he's trailing a running bird, which he might flush out of gun range. Similarly, if he takes off chasing a deer, coyote, bobcat, badger, wolverine, or such, you stop him with the *Sit*-whistle, in some cases to save him from injury. In waterfowling and dog-games, whenever you must handle him at a distance, whether on a blind or on a mark, you must first stop him with the *Sit*-whistle. In short, the *Sit*-whistle is the *sine qua non* (without which there is nothing) for control.

Granted, you could teach your dog to sit when you toot "Way Down Upon the Suwannee River" on your whistle—or any other series of sounds that appeals to you. However, since the *Sit*-whistle is the most important whistle command in your repertoire, common sense demands that it be the simplest, the easiest to blow, and therefore the most difficult for your dog to misunderstand. That's why experienced retriever trainers have so long reserved the single, sharp blast for the *Sit*-whistle, using various multiple-toned warblings for other, less urgent commands. (Traditionally, they use the following: one long and two shorts, drawn out gently—*Tweeeee-twee-twee*—for

Come-in; and two notes, blown softly and rapidly—*pip-pip*—to turn a dog quartering in the uplands.)

TEACHING IT IS EASY—TOO EASY

Teaching a dog to stop on the whistle is so easy that "slipped whistles" should be extremely rare. ("Slipped whistle" is a euphemism for "whistle refusal" or "ignored whistle.") However, they are very common, at least in dog-games where everyone sees them and judges count them. I suspect they are even more common in hunting, where all a dog's mistakes are forgotten after he picks up the bird.

Most people teach their puppies to sit very early, perhaps as soon as the pup is comfortable in his new environment. And puppies pick this up

Young Tyler Wilson uses a food treat to induce his Lab puppy, "Chance" (Wilson's Last Chance), to sit.

so easily. By the time a pup is three months old, the proud owner is showing off how reliably his pup sits on command for family members, neighbors, and visitors. Many such puppy owners extend this training quite early to sitting in response to a whistle command . . . or "sitting on the whistle," as we normally call it (without picturing what that would involve if taken literally).

The pup quickly and easily learns to sit on both the verbal command and the *Sit*-whistle anywhere in the house or backyard. Trouble is, the owner thinks he has finished with this training, when in reality he has only begun. Being human and easily bored, he moves on to more challenging training, like play retrieving, obedience, field work, perhaps force-breaking, and so on. Seldom does he toot the *Sit*-whistle for his youngster, and when he does it's always in the house or backyard. And the dog responds, so what's to worry?

Much later on, in blind retrieve training, his now-mature retriever begins to slip whistles, and gets away with it. In a training session once, I watched a person overlook more than 35 combined whistle and cast refusals on a single blind retrieve. (I stopped counting at 35 and the dog wasn't halfway there yet!) When the dog finally stumbled onto the bird, the "trainer" was so delighted he forgot that the dog had been out of control from the get-go. That was an extreme case, but most beginners tend to forget whistle refusals as soon as their dogs pick up the bird. Then, in dog-games, where the judges neither overlook nor forget anything (good or bad), these same beginners have difficulty accepting how poorly their dogs score. Many go into a form of denial—"Hey! He got the bird, didn't he? What else matters?" (This last question has a simple answer: "Control matters!")

If the initial steps in teaching the Sit-*whistle were more difficult, most beginners would devote more time to it, and thereby do a more complete job of it.*

So, to uncomplicate life when you get into real blind retrieves, resolve not only to teach your pup to sit on the whistle around the house from his earliest days, but also to extend and maintain that training throughout your training program. Maintaining it is as easy as teaching it, but a lot less exciting. When you first teach a pup *anything*, the success is exhilarating. Later on, maintaining it can become rather ho-hum—to you, but not to your dog. Dogs, lacking human intelligence, don't suffer boredom nearly as quickly as we do.

TEACHING A PUP—OR AN OLDER DOG—
TO *SIT* ON THE WHISTLE

Through the years, several techniques for teaching a dog this elementary skill have been developed and documented. As far as I know, they all work! Here I'll tell you the unoriginal way in which I do it. If you are already attached to another method that has worked for you, do it that way. However, if you are a beginner, you should follow some method that has worked for others rather than indulging your creative urges in this all-important command.

After a new puppy is settled in at our place and has bonded with me, I teach him his name (and *No!*, of course). Then I accustom him to a little puppy strap collar and the restraint he feels from a lead. With that behind us, I put him on lead in the backyard and play with him awhile. Now and then, I interrupt the play with a clearly enunciated command *Sit*. At first he has no idea what this means, so I guide him into a sitting position by pushing his fanny down with one hand while I hold his muzzle up with the other. As soon as he's sitting, I praise him soothingly and give him a dog-treat. I hold him in a sitting position a few seconds, then release my grip as I give him a clearly enunciated release command (I use *Okay*). Teaching *Sit* forces me to also teach *Okay*, so the pup will know when he is "on command" and when he is again free to do as he pleases (within normal societal limitations, of course).

I repeat this several times per session. Eventually, through the conditioning that results from rote drilling, the pup will sit on command without any help from me—for which he continues to get praise and, at least sometimes, a treat. Next, I introduce the whistle. I say *Sit*, and as he is doing so, I toot the *Sit*-whistle. I call this "training by association," for I toot the *Sit*-whistle when he is already in the act of sitting. His little canine thinker quickly associates this new whistle command with his act of sitting. After a few successful repetitions, I toot the *Sit*-whistle without the verbal command. If he looks confused, I help him into a sitting position—then praise him and give him a treat. As soon as he understands the whistle command, I mix it in with the verbal command, so he will learn to sit on either. However, I use the *Sit*-whistle probably 80 percent of the time, because that's the one I will rely on the most for the rest of his life.

Next, I walk him around the yard, on lead. Periodically I toot the *Sit*-whistle. Then I use the lead to guide him around so he is facing me as he sits down. If he has any difficulty, I help him into a sitting position facing me—then I praise him and give him a treat. Through the next several sessions, I command him to sit while he is farther and farther away from me (but still on a six-foot lead). If he tries to come to me before sitting, which is common, I move him back to where he should have sat, put him in a sitting position, and praise and treat him. Then I step back to where I was when I tooted the whistle, stand there, and toot it again. He's already sitting, so I praise him from this distance. Then I step toward him, give him a treat, and step back again before releasing him.

When he sits reliably at the end of the six-foot lead, I start using a retractable lead, which allows me to extend this training to greater distances. I prefer the retractable lead to a rope because it allows me to keep the line between the dog and me reasonably taut. It doesn't fall to the ground, where it can tangle around the dog's legs—and mine.

When he does well in the backyard, I begin to take him, still on the retractable lead, for walks around the neighborhood. This brings all sorts of distractions into the game. Now and then (but not more often than every five minutes), when he is totally distracted by something, and perhaps tugging on the retractable lead, I toot the *Sit*-whistle and, if necessary, enforce compliance (gently). Then I praise him and give him a treat. After a few days of these daily walks, he sits nicely in spite of the various distractions we encounter around the neighborhood.

Then I extend this training to the field. After each field training session, I snap the retractable lead on him and take him for a walk. Now and then, when he is distracted (by anything but a bird), I toot the *Sit*-whistle and, if necessary, enforce compliance. I also gradually reduce the food treats and rely more and more on praise alone. By this time, praise should be enough of a reward. Besides, to give him a food treat, I must walk to where he's sitting. In a dog's simple mind, a delayed reward has little meaning.

The process for training an older dog to sit on the whistle—a dog that was not so trained as a pup—is the same. He will pick it up more quickly—that's the good news—and ignore the whistle more quickly if he is not drilled thoroughly. Thus, you should spend about as much time on this initial drilling with the older dog as you do with a pup.

Extending the *Sit*-whistle to the field. Here, during a post-training romp, the author has blown the *Sit*-whistle. Both Beaver (Chessy) and Rhett (Golden) promptly sat.

MAINTAINING *SIT*-WHISTLE TRAINING

Eventually, I omit the retractable lead and toot the *Sit*-whistle—but I do this first in the backyard, where the pup will be easier to catch if necessary. I also start out when he's rather close to me. Normally, he sits automatically. If not, I enforce compliance and then return to my position, repeat the whistle and praise him. Then I release him.

As his responses allow, I extend the distance between us, but I stay in the backyard until I can stop him anywhere there, with neither refusal nor slow response. Then, I take him off-lead out in the field, and repeat the process, starting when he is close to me and not distracted, and building from there.

Thereafter, for the rest of the dog's active life, after most regular field training sessions, I cut him loose for a romp and let him run. Periodically, I toot the *Sit*-whistle. By now, I shouldn't have to worry about refusals. If he ignores the whistle now, I've pushed him too rapidly and should go back a few spaces. However, I may have to deal with slow responses from time to time, which will be discussed a little further on.

Extending the *Stop*-whistle to water. Here, Marilyn Corbin has stopped her Golden, Summer, in the middle of a small pond.

"SITTING" IN WATER

In hunting, most blind retrieves occur in waterfowling, and therefore in water. In dog-games the blind retrieves are about equally divided between land and water. Thus, whether you are a dog-gamer or a hunter, you must train your dog to respond to the *Sit*-whistle in water as well as on land. Of course, a dog can't actually "sit" in swimming water. Instead, he should simply turn to face you, so you can give him an appropriate cast. Thus, the term "*Stop*-whistle" may be more appropriate in water work.

How do you teach your dog to obey the *Stop*-whistle in water? Stated quite simply, you can't! Actually, you shouldn't *teach* anything in water. You should teach on land and then extend what you have thusly taught into water. The better you train your dog to respond to the *Sit*-whistle on land, the better he will respond to it in water. If, after having approached it this way, you find your dog is beginning to slip whistles while swimming, you should correct him with the e-collar, as described in the next section.

DEALING WITH SLIPPED WHISTLES
AND SLOW RESPONSES

Frankly, before the electronic collar, slipped whistles and slow responses were a plague for most trainers. If the trainer ran out to the dog, the dog would probably sit long before the huffing and puffing humanoid arrived, so immediate correction was impossible. (To maintain this book's GP rating, I won't go into the long-range correction "tools" some used before the e-collar.) Today, thanks to the modern e-collar, a person can deal effectively and humanely with almost any problem at a distance, *once the dog is collar-conditioned.* Slipped whistles and slow responses are especially easy to correct: Zap the dog at an appropriate level of continuous stimulation until his tush touches *terra firma.* When he's sitting as he should be, end the stimulation and praise him. If you correct him this way consistently, his responses will improve and quicken as if by magic.

BE PERSISTENT

Most of the combination drills in Chapter 9 drill the dog in stopping as well as lining and/or casting. However, we don't have the elaborate array of drills specifically designed to keep a dog sharp on the *Sit*-whistle. We don't have them because we don't need them! Sitting on the whistle is so easy to teach and so easy to maintain that no one has had to invent elaborate drills to facilitate the process.

But, you've got to work on it regularly if you hope to maintain your dog's responses at an acceptable level. Those romps after regular training sessions, with occasional *Sit*-whistles, will work wonders—if you let them. If you put them off regularly, instead of doing them regularly, your dog's responses will deteriorate, perhaps rapidly, perhaps slowly, but surely.

So work at the *Sit*-whistle a little while after every training session—persistently.

TO GET YOUR DOG TO LOOK AT YOU

When you are handling your dog to a blind retrieve, after you stop him, you give him a cast, typically with an arm signal. If your dog doesn't look at you, he can't see your arm signal. *Ergo*, you can't cast him. Some dogs play this game quite willfully, in that they refuse to look at their handler because they don't want to take his casts. Instead, they want to go wherever they choose. When this happens in hunting or in a dog-game, instead of giving your dog a cast, you should toot the *Sit*-whistle again—and again and again, if necessary, until he looks at you. It makes no sense to cast him when he's not looking.

Repeating the *Sit*-whistle is about all you can do in such situations. However, you can add a little wrinkle to your *Sit*-whistle maintenance training that will prevent such situations from coming up. During your dog's post-training romps, carry a dummy in your vest

Getting your stopped retriever to look at you. Here, the author has stopped his Golden, Gamble, and is about to toss a dummy for him to retrieve. *Photo by Mary Jo Gallagher.*

where he can't see it. If you were to carry it in your hand, where he could see it all the time, he might not leave your side. Let him romp, and stop him with the whistle periodically. After he sits on the whistle, toss the dummy and send him to retrieve it. If you do this consistently during these romps, every time he sits he will focus his entire attention on you—because he knows you are about to toss a dummy for him.

In fact, whenever you stop him fairly close to you, you can turn this into a form of the "baseball" casting drill. After he stops, consider him to be on the pitcher's mound and yourself to be at home plate. Toss the dummy to any of the three bases, or to the "bunt" position between him and yourself. Then, cast him to the dummy. By doing this, you condition him both to lock in on you when he sits on the whistle and to take your casts after stopping at a distance. Of course, you can do this only when you stop him reasonably close to you, so you can toss the dummy to any of the bases. But, at any distance, you can toss a dummy *somewhere* and send him for it with your normal command to retrieve.

Photo courtesy of Bobbie Christensen.

7
Casting
Concepts

HANDLING TECHNIQUES

The Four Basic Casts

After you have lined your dog toward the bird in a blind retrieve, if he veers off toward the boundary of the fairway, or if he begins to potter around, you should stop him and redirect him. You redirect him by giving him a "cast"—with an arm signal and either a whistle or voice command, plus perhaps a little body English. The four basic casts, which all retriever handlers use, are as follows: *Over* (to the left); *Over* (to the right); *Back* (straight away from the handler); and *Come-in* (toward the handler).

Over! (Left or Right)

You give this cast by pumping the appropriate forearm (left arm for left-*Over*, right arm for right-*Over*) horizontally at shoulder height one or more times as you walk in the appropriate direction, and say the command word *Over!* This sounds simple. However, these basic *Over* casts have some subtleties of which you should be aware. For example, keeping your arm horizontal at shoulder height isn't as easy as it sounds. If you extend it with your palm toward your dog—your thumb at the top of your hand—and pump your arm from the elbow as you should, your arm will almost certainly drift upward. But, with your hand reversed (palm away from your dog and your thumb at the bottom of

"Over!"

your hand), your arm will tend naturally to remain horizontal as you pump it.

So, rule #1 for the two *Over* casts is: *Thumbs down!*

If, while giving an *Over* cast with one arm, you don't control your other arm, it may flap around in the breeze. With both your arms waving about, your dog won't know what you expect him to do.

So, rule #2 for *Over* casts is: *Tuck the inactive arm in tightly against your tummy!*

In training, you should give *Over* casts the same way every time, for three reasons: to help your dog understand what you want; to help yourself form good handling habits; and to facilitate effective use, later on in hunting and dog-games, of appropriate variations in the way you give *Over* casts (see rule #4, below).

So, rule #3 is: *In training, give your* Over *casts calmly and deliberately. Don't rush, and don't tarry. Pump your arm purposefully. Step smoothly. Say "Over!" clearly and deliberately.*

After your dog is fully trained, he will become quite sensitive to variations in the how you give *Over* casts. In general, there are three "levels" of *Over* casts: normal, "hard," and "soft." The normal level is the one you use in training all the time, as well as the one you should use probably 80 to 90 percent of the time in hunting and dog-games. However, you will sometimes be able to use hard and soft *Over*s to advantage.

To give a hard *Over*, do everything more vigorously than normal: Pump your arm rapidly, step quickly, and shout *Over!* When you do this, your dog will start *Over* and then quickly scallop *Back*—and the "harder" the *Over*, the more quickly he will scallop *Back*. He will do this naturally, with no special training. In fact, you should not use hard *Over*s in training, lest you diminish this natural inclination. Save it for hunting and dog-games, where it will occasionally serve you well. For example, let's say you have stopped your dog a tad to the right of the true line to the bird. Let's also say that, if you were to give him a straight *Back*, he would probably pass the bird on the upwind side, which would force you to stop and cast him again near the bird. However, if, instead of a straight *Back*, you give him an extremely hard left *Over*, he would almost certainly swing far enough left before scalloping *Back* to put himself on a line that will take him immediately downwind of the bird, where his nose would do the rest. In such a case, the hard left *Over* would be well justified.

To give a soft *Over*, pump your arm gently, step slowly, and say *Over* softly (or even, in extreme cases, remain silent). When would a soft *Over* come in handy? Let's say, in a dog-game, you've just stopped your dog immediately after he has missed an angled entry into water and has started running down the shoreline. To keep him "alive" in the dog-game, you must put him into the water immediately with, let's say, a right *Over*. But, since he has already avoided the water, you know his mind-set is such that a normal right *Over* will probably drive him farther down the shoreline instead of into the water. So you give him a soft *Over*. You slow everything down. You move your arm cautiously; you step lightly; and you either say *Over* softly or not at all. Like magic, your dog will almost surely take the cast and jump into the drink rather than scallop back to continue running the bank. This, too, is a natural tendency, not something you must train for. (Here's a little trick for extremely critical situations: Combine a very soft *Over* cast with a gentle, almost pleading, *Come-in* whistle! That will normally surprise your dog into taking the *Over* instead of scalloping back, because the *Come-in* whistle strongly counteracts his inclination to go *Back*. However, to maintain the element of surprise, never do this in training. In fact, use it most sparingly in hunting and dog-games. *"If the salt loses its savor . . ."*)

So, rule #4 for *Over* casts is: *To maximize your dog's performance in hunting and dog-games, use normal, hard, and soft* Overs *appropriately.*

Back!

When you need to send your dog straight away from you, you give him a *Back!* cast. To do this, place the palm of one hand (either one) on the corresponding thigh, stiffen your arm, and swing your hand straight forward in a semicircle to a position high above your head. To learn this gesture, stand with your arm straight down in front of you and the palm of your hand on your thigh. Stiffen your arm at the elbow. Now swing your hand to the front as if you were about to make a Nazi salute (sorry!), but continue swinging it up until your hand is as high as you can comfortably reach above your head. Many beginners tend to stop the hand at shoulder level, because it is then pointing in the direction they want the dog to go. However, from any distance, the dog cannot see either the hand or the arm in that position.

If you don't stiffen your arm, it will often drift sideways as you bring it up. This lateral movement can cause the dog to start *Over* immediately without waiting to see the complete *Back* cast. This happens especially when the dog's mind-set at the moment is to go over rather than back.

So, rule #1 for *Back* casts is: *With a stiff arm, swing your hand in a forward semicircle from your thigh to a position high above your head.*

If, while giving a *Back* cast with one arm, you let the other arm flap in the breeze, said other arm may give your dog a conflicting cast.

So, rule #2 for *Back* casts is: *Tuck the opposite arm in tightly against your tummy.*

"Back!"

With which arm should you give a *Back* cast? When your dog has been on an *Over* cast, and you now want to send him *Back*, you should "change arms." If he has been running a right-arm *Over*, give him a left-arm *Back*, and *vice versa*. Why? For some reason, if you give him a left-arm *Back* after a left-arm *Over* or a right-arm *Back* after a right-arm *Over*, he will most likely continue the *Over* rather than take the *Back*. Maybe not every time, but often enough to make not changing arms foolish.

So, rule #3 for *Back* casts is: *When going from an* Over *to a* Back, *change arms.*

When you aren't going from an *Over* to a *Back*, you should base your "which arm?" decision on a combination of factors. First, have you trained him to turn in the direction of the arm you use? If not, which way does he turn when sent back? Where is your dog relative to the bird? And where are the hazards?

If you have trained him to "turn with your arm," that is, to spin to the left when you give him a left-arm *Back* and to spin to the right when you give him a right-arm *Back*, you should use the arm that will turn him in the most favorable, or less risky, direction. If a major hazard (such as a point of land in a water blind) awaits him on one side, by all means turn him away from that hazard. You will occasionally encounter a situation in which, to keep your dog out of trouble, you will not only use the arm that turns him away from the hazard, but you will even give him a hard *Over* rather than a *Back*.

If you have not trained your dog to turn with your arm, he will consistently turn either to the left or to the right, regardless of which arm you use. That being the case, you should use the arm—and the cast—that will most surely keep him out of trouble, given the hazards involved. If, for example, he always turns to the right and the hazard is on the right, you should use your left arm, and perhaps even give him a hard left *Over* (to turn him away from the hazard before he scallops back) instead of a *Back*. But, if the trouble is on the left, you should give him a right-arm *Back*.

So, rule #4 for *Back* casts is: *When not going from an* Over *to a* Back, *choose the arm that will most likely steer your dog away from trouble.*

Come-In!

To bring a dog in toward you with a *Come-in* cast, toot the *Come-in* whistle (*Tweeeee-twee-twee*) with what has become the traditional body English—stoop a little, squat a little, and extend one or both hands, with palms out, straight down toward the ground.

One may question how much this time-honored body English contributes to the success of the cast—beyond giving the handler a sense of involvement. However, because so many retrieverites have performed this ceremonial dance at the line for so many years, most of us would find not doing it too, too uncomfortable. Besides, it does no harm. In fact, by moving laterally as we stoop, squat, and drag our knuckles on the ground, we can actually steer our dogs this way or that as they come

"Come-in!"

toward us. (Far be it from me to experiment to determine whether moving laterally in a more upright, humanoid stance would accomplish the same thing!)

The *Come-in* cast has only one "rule": If your dog is too far out, bring him in closer with the *Come-in* whistle, accompanied by whatever body English you find comfortable—or comforting.

Angled Casts

All retriever trainers teach their dogs the above four basic casts. Many also teach the four "angled" casts that fall between each pair of the basic casts. The angled casts are: left- and right-angled *Back*, left- and right-angled *Come-in*.

To give an angled *Back*, raise the appropriate hand on a stiff arm to a position halfway between its position for a *Back* and an *Over*, that is, halfway between vertical and horizontal. Then step in that direction and command *Back!* To give an angled *Come-in* cast, extend the appropriate arm halfway between its position for an *Over* and a *Come-in*, that is, halfway between horizontal and straight down. Then step in that direction as you blow the *Come-in* whistle. (A slight squat is traditional and proper, but not required, for angled *Come-ins*.)

Like almost everything else in retriever training, angled casts were invented by field trial pros. And like almost everything else invented by field trial pros, angled casts were developed to help them win. Doing good solid work is not, and has never been, enough to win trials. To win, a dog must perform *better* than his competition. In blind retrieves, "the straightest line to the bird is the best job." Clearly, the straightest line requires the fewest "whistles" (number of times the handler must stop and cast his dog). In a properly executed angled cast, one whistle does the work of two. Without the angle, the handler would have to give his dog two whistles: one for an *Over*, and the other for either a *Back* or a *Come-in*. Since the angled cast sends the dog on a path halfway between those two casts, it accomplishes the same thing with only one whistle. Small wonder you see such a monotony of angled casts in field trials!

However, angled casts substantially increase the risk of a refusal, because the angled cast attempts to send the dog on a line dangerously close to the one he was taking when stopped. Let's say your dog is heading toward the blind on a good line, but then drifts off to the left for some reason. So you stop him. If you give him a right-*Over*, you strongly counteract his tendency to drift left. Then, if you let him carry that *Over* a little past the true line to the blind, you give him a little "drifting room" for the subsequent *Back* cast. This combination of two casts will give you a good job with minimal risk of refusals. If, instead, you opt for an angled cast (here a right-angled *Back*)—*and if he takes it*—you will have a better job. However, unlike the *Over*, the angled cast does not—cannot—strongly counteract whatever was influencing the dog to drift left. Thus, he may well, as they say, "thumb his nose at you" and continue drifting left. In field trial language, that's a "cast refusal." After such a refusal, you'll have to stop him again very quickly. (Right then, you have two whistles and a cast refusal, which is much worse than the two whistles and no refusals you would have had with the *Over* followed by a *Back*.)

Thus, angled casts are like the little girl in the old nursery rhyme, the one with the little curl right in the middle of her forehead: When angled casts are good, they're very, very good, but when they're bad, they're horrid. Even so, in competitive field trials, handlers often must gamble this way, if they hope to win.

The situation in hunt tests is totally different, because hunt tests are noncompetitive. You can earn every hunt test title available without ever "beating" anyone. If your dog does the work, he qualifies, regardless of how well or how poorly the other dogs happened to do. If he fails to do the work, he does not qualify, again regardless of what the other dogs may have done. So, let's put on our "hunt test glasses" and take another look at the above situation in which your dog was drifting left. If you play it safe and give him the right-*Over* followed by a *Back*, he will almost certainly take both casts and do a creditable job. If you risk the right-angled *Back—and if he takes it*—you'll have an even better job. *But so what?* Either way, you'll receive the same orange qualifying rosette. So you have gambled for absolutely nothing!

But, if he refuses the angled cast, you must stop him again very quickly. As mentioned above, that's two whistles and one cast refusal—much worse than the two whistles and no refusals you'd have with the right-*Over* and *Back*. When you stop him after the angled *Back* refusal, unless you are a cooler handler than some hunt testers I've judged, you may well panic and repeat the angled *Back*. Only this time, you'll put some real emotion into both your voice and your arm signal. That, of course, will drive him, not into the angled *Back*, but straight *Back* and into his former drift to the left. Another refusal. And so on until the dog goes completely out of control. It happens—and it's so unnecessary.

I've often thought that hunt test clubs would pass out a lot more qualifying rosettes if angled casts were outlawed. They won't be, and really shouldn't be. But, if handlers would analyze rationally how best to cope with the hunt test noncompetitive environment—instead of (to be brutally blunt) mindlessly imitating field trialers—a person would seldom see an angled cast in hunt tests. .

Do angled casts have any place in actual hunting? Well, not any *rational* place, of course, because reducing two whistles to one has no advantage in hunting situations. However, angled casts may have an *emotional* place for some hunters. Some people just like to be different, even if it means doing everything the hard way. (I once knew a guy who golfed left-handed cross-handed and, compared to his convoluted swing, this grip looked downright orthodox! He shot consistently in the low 200s, and was perfectly happy with his scores as long as his style of play attracted sufficient attention—which it did, believe me, especially among the following foursomes for whom he held up play.)

Chapter 8 explains how to train your dog to take angled casts, if such is your wish. However, before you spend the requisite time on such drills, you should analyze whether the benefits of angled casts *for you* justify the time and effort involved.

Let me throw one other little-known fact into your analysis: Even if you never train your dog on angled casts, by the time he's running real blind retrieves well, he'll take them naturally almost as well as he would with extensive training! Years ago, when I was running in field trials in a small way, I never trained my dogs in angled casts. Yet, they took them naturally. Nor was this unusual. Back then, as far as I know, no one actually trained for angled casts, but almost everyone used them. Training for them seems to be a relatively recent refinement, one that has added a small amount of reliability and polish—but only after a significant investment of training time.

TURNING WITH YOUR ARM

The Decision

On *Back* casts, if left to his own devices, each dog will form a habit of turning just one way as he leaves his sitting position. Some dogs always turn to the handler's left; others always turn to his right. (Throughout this section, "left" and "right" always refer to the handler's left or right, not the dog's.) The direction in which a dog turns has some effect on how you should handle him. For example, the dog that always turn to the right will carry his *Back* casts on a line to the right of the one he would take if he always turned left. Thus, if you stop a right-turning dog while he's running a left-to-right *Over*, you should stop him a bit short of the true line to the bird, to allow his turn to put him on a collision course with the bird. Conversely, if you stop him while he's running a right-to-left *Over*, you should let him overrun the true line a little, to allow his turn to bring him back to the true line. As you grow accustomed to handling such a dog, you'll come to make such compensations without thinking about it.

However, if you were a pro handling ten or twelve dogs, you would have trouble remembering which one turns left and which one turns right. And, if you were a field trial pro, trying to win in tough competition, and needing to fine-tune your handling, having some dogs turn left and other dogs turn right would cost you placements, and therefore

When Mary Jo Gallagher gives Fortune a left-arm *Back*, he turns to her left.

When Mary Jo Gallagher gives Fortune a right-arm *Back*, he turns to her right.

customers and money. Small wonder then that field trial pros long ago began training their dogs to turn left when the boss raises his left mitt for a *Back* cast, and to turn right when he raises his right. That way, in trials, he can handle all the dogs in his string without having to remember which way each one turns.

True enough, a pro could accomplish this by teaching all his dogs to turn the same way, either right or left, all the time. However, that requires almost as much work as teaching them to "turn with his arm." Besides, in many ticklish field trial situations, a handler finds it helpful to be able to turn his dog this way or that, simply by raising the appropriate arm. (Similarly, field trialers teach their dogs to heel and therefore to work from both sides. In some tests, dogs that work from the left have an advantage; in other tests, the advantage goes to dogs working from the right. If your dog will work from either side, you have the best of both worlds.)

If you are training several dogs, especially for field trials, you should definitely teach each of them to "turn with your arm." However, if you are training only one or two dogs, and not for field trials, you should ponder this decision carefully. Will you gain enough from it to justify the training time you will have to expend? Would that time be better spent in other areas? Only you can decide.

The Training

If you decide to teach this little refinement, the younger your dog is when you start, the easier the training will be. Regardless of his age, you should complete it early in his casting work, so you don't have to overcome established habits.

Start out using a long barrier (wall or fence) to prevent the dog from turning the wrong way. Have him sit with, say, his left shoulder tight against the barrier. Toss a dummy a few feet behind him. Now give him a left-arm *Back* (for which he must turn to *his* right, *your* left). As you raise your left arm, step slightly to your left to suggest motion in that direction to him. Repeat this several times. Then flip-flop the entire setup so he is sitting with his right shoulder tight against the barrier, and repeat the drill with a right-arm *Back* (stepping to your right as you do). Repeat this drill through several sessions, using as many different barriers as you can.

When you are sure he has formed the habit of turning with your arm, work him without a barrier. At first, use a long buggy whip to guide him into the proper turn. Stand close enough to him so you can reach him with the buggy whip. Hold it in, say, your right hand, with the tip beside him. Now, give him a left-arm *Back*. As you do, step to your left and tap him (lightly, please!) with the buggy whip on his opposite shoulder. That will steer him into the proper turn. Repeat several times. Then change locations and switch to a right-arm *Back*, handling the buggy whip with your left hand. Eventually, you will be able to remain in one location and intersperse the two casts, always handling the buggy whip with the opposite hand. With enough of this drill, your dog will learn to key off of your arm, and turn with it.

Baseball

In his 1949 book, *Training Your Retriever*, the late James Lamb Free used a baseball analogy to explain how to teach three of the basic casts (both *Over*s and *Back*). He said that the Hogan family of professional trainers had taught him this concept. Picture a baseball diamond, with the dog sitting on the pitcher's mound, the handler standing at home plate, and dummies at the three bases. When the handler gives a left-*Over* cast, the dog retrieves the dummy at third base; on a right-*Over* cast, he retrieves the dummy at first base; on a *Back* cast, he retrieves the dummy at second base. Although Mr. Free failed to include the *Come-in* cast, you can easily add it without departing from the baseball analogy. Simply picture it as a bunt straight back toward the mound. Since the publication of that book, most casting drills have been named "baseball" of this or that type: visual aid baseball; two-dummy baseball; walking baseball; and so on. Although Mr. Free's original baseball scheme was indeed a drill, it lives on mostly as the concept which underlies most subsequent casting drills. For this reason, I'll describe it briefly here.

In the Free drill, after laying out a "diamond" on bare ground or closely clipped grass, the trainer first teaches each cast individually. With his dog sitting on the pitcher's mound, he carries several dummies to the intended location (first base, second base, third base, or bunt position) and drops them there while the dog watches. Then he walks to home plate and gives his dog the appropriate cast. Since the animal watched the trainer drop the dummies, he will take the cast and retrieve

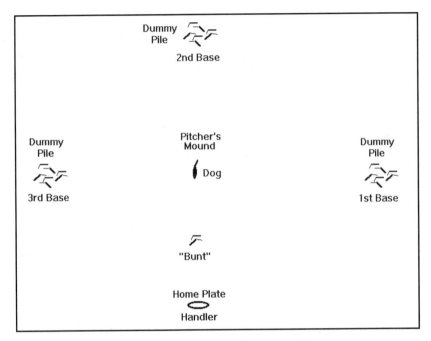

Figure 15. Basic Baseball Casting Drill.

one of the dummies. Next, the trainer heels the dog back to the pitcher's mound and leaves him sitting there. He returns to home plate and repeats the same cast. Although, this time, the dog didn't see the dummies dropped immediately before this cast, he'll remember where they are and will again take the cast. And so on for the remaining dummies.

After the dog knows all four casts individually, the trainer starts combining them in opposite pairs (first and third bases, or second base and the bunt position). After the dog handles these pairs well, the trainer puts dummies at all four locations and mixes up the casts randomly. After the dog takes all four casts on bare ground, the trainer moves his diamond into cover, where he gradually lengthens the casts.

That's all there is to it. These days we have several much more effective techniques for training a dog to take casts, but they all trace back to this ingenious program of Martin Hogan, who happily taught it to Mr. Free, who included it in his book, which has become a classic (and is still in print after all these decades).

8
Casting
Drills

This chapter contains five drills that are purely for casting. (Chapter 9 contains drills that combine casting with one or both of the other two parts of the blind retrieve.) Three of the drills in this chapter—visual aid baseball with the four basic casts; visual aid baseball with all eight casts; and two-dummy baseball—are "teaching" drills for introducing a retriever to casting. One drill—visual aid baseball in water—is an "extension" drill, for extending the casting concept from land into water. The fifth drill—D. L.'s walking baseball—is a "polishing" drill for keeping the trained retriever's casting sharp.

DRILLS

Visual Aid Baseball with the Four Basic Casts

Description

This trial-and-success drill augments and extends James Lamb Free's basic baseball drill (see Chapter 7) by means of visual aids at the three bases and at the bunt station. Visual aids facilitate the initial learning steps, especially for those who are also using them for lining drills. Visual aids also facilitate extending this casting drill into cover, through various hazards, and even into water. In each new situation, the trainer first casts his dog to each visual once or twice. Then he removes the visual aids and casts him again to each dummy pile a couple of times. That way, the dog succeeds initially because of the visual aids, then later because he remembers where the dummy piles are. Enough of this type

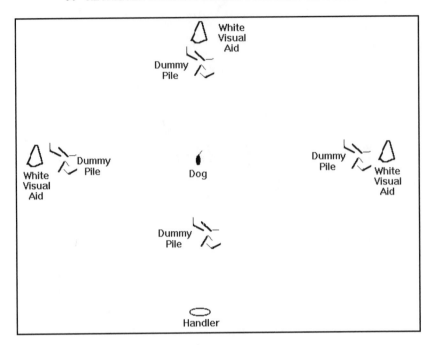

Figure 16. Visual Aid Baseball Drill.

of drill will condition him to take the trainer's casts automatically, even in real blind retrieves.

Purpose of Drill

Initially, this drill enables you to introduce your dog to casting in a most positive way. Then, later on, it allows you to extend this training to all manner of hazards. You can and should use this drill all through your dog's active life—for teaching, maintenance, and "refresher courses."

Prerequisites

Your dog should be well started in the visual aid lining drill before beginning this casting drill. That way, he'll understand the intent of the visual aids.

Equipment and Facilities

You need three or four visual aids of the same type as those you use in the visual aid lining drill. (If you plan to use a visual aid regularly at the bunt station, you need four visual aids. Otherwise, you can get by with three.) You need enough dummies for a pile at each station, typically six dummies per pile. Ideally, you should have dummies of four different colors. If you put a specific color at each station, you can keep better track of how many dummies are left in each pile, by counting how many of that color your dog has already retrieved.

You need suitable training grounds. Initially, you should work in a flat, bare-ground or closely clipped grass area large enough to allow you to extend your dog's casts out to at least 50 yards. Later, you will do this drill in the various types of cover, terrain, and other hazards you normally train in.

Precautions and Pitfalls

Avoid casting your dog to a station which no longer has any dummies. This confuses the dog, especially early in this training. To avoid this, use a specific color of dummies for each station—say, white for first base, black for second, red for third, and gray for the bunt position. Put out the same number of dummies (say, six) at each station. As your dog retrieves dummies to you, toss them behind you into piles separated by color. That allows you to tell at a glance whether any station is devoid of dummies.

Don't overwork your dog in any one session.

Process—Steps in Training

You should first teach each cast individually, then begin combining them. In a flat, bare-ground area, lay out your baseball diamond with each cast only about fifteen yards long. Put out no dummies yet. First, put a visual aid only at second base (*Back* cast). Heel your dog to the mound and have him sit there. Now carry six dummies to the visual aid (at second base). Make sure your dog watches as you drop them there, one at a time. Walk back to home plate and give him a *Back* cast. Since he just watched you drop the dummies, he'll spin and head for the dummy pile.

After he delivers to you at home plate, toss the dummy behind you, then heel him back to the mound, and have him sit there again. Return to home plate and cast him *Back* again. He may hesitate this time, for you didn't drop the dummies there immediately before this cast. If he does, walk toward him, repeating the command encouragingly as you do. He'll catch on and run to the dummy pile. When he reaches it (not before), praise him lavishly. Repeat this *Back* cast for the remaining four dummies. It may take two or three such sessions before he becomes comfortable with the *Back* cast. (Since it's the most difficult, and the most frequently used in real blind retrieves, you should teach it first.) Stay with it alone until you feel he has it down quite well.

Next, introduce the opposite cast, the *Come-in*. Start the session with two or three *Back* casts to the dummy pile and visual aid at second base. Then move the visual aid and all the dummies to the bunt position, between the mound and home plate. (Leave nothing at second base.) With your dog on the mound and watching, drop the six dummies by the visual aid. Return to home plate and give him a *Come-in* cast. He should run in, pick up a dummy and bring it to you. Then repeat this cast for the other five dummies. Do two or three sessions like this, always starting with two or three *Back* casts, followed by six *Come-ins*. (If you wish, you can stop putting the visual aid at the bunt position after one or two sessions. Since your dog is looking right at that dummy pile as he faces you on the mound, he shouldn't need the additional "guidance." Of course, don't leave the visual aid at second base, where it would confuse your dog. Instead, put it away, out of sight.) At this stage, don't put dummies at both stations. With dummies at only one station, even if he goes the wrong way, he won't find anything to retrieve.

Next, introduce one of the *Over* casts, following the same general procedure. Start off with a couple of *Back* casts, followed by a couple of *Come-ins*. Then move the visual aid to first or third base, and drop the dummies there, one at a time, while your dog watches from the mound. (Of course, you should make sure no dummies remain at either second base or the bunt position, in case he makes a mistake.) After he understands this cast, which may take two or three sessions, introduce the opposite *Over* cast the same way.

Now that he knows all four casts individually, begin to pair them up. Before getting your dog out of his dog-box, put a visual aid and a dummy pile at second base and a dummy pile at the bunt position (with or without a visual aid, whichever you prefer.) Now heel your dog to the mound, making sure he sees the visual aid at second base. Walk to home plate and give him a *Back* cast. Next, give him a *Come-in*. Thereafter, mix the two casts up unpredictably, so he won't establish a fixed pattern.

Repeat with the two *Over* casts (but not including either the *Back* or the *Come-in*). After he can handle all four casts in opposite pairs, you can safely put out all four dummy piles, with visual aids at least at the three bases. Cast him to each of them several times, but in no fixed sequence. Since the *Back* cast is both most difficult, you should give him as many *Back*s as you give him other casts combined. Cast him twice each to first base, third base, and to the bunt pile, but six times to second base—in random order, of course. That's twelve casts, which is plenty for one session.

Next, while still on bare ground, lengthen his casts out until his *Overs* are 50 yards, his *Come-in* 25 yards, and his *Back* at least 75 yards. Also, give him only one cast to each station with the visual aid in place. Then, remove the visual aids and complete the drill without them. Reduce the total number of casts to compensate for the greater distances, lest you overwork him.

Thereafter, move into cover—but shorten up initially, of course. Cast him once or twice to each station with the visual aids in place. Rest him a few minutes while you pick the visual aids up. Then complete the drill without them.

Introduce various hazards—rolling terrain, ditches, tire-track roads in the pasture, cover changes, and so forth—the same way. Run him first with the visual aids in place, then without them.

Addenda

As is shown below, this visual aid baseball drill can be extended easily into water. But you shouldn't do that until your dog is thoroughly trained in it on land.

Later, in real blind retrieves, whenever your dog's casts become sloppy—as they will from time to time—take him back to bare ground with long casts to visual aid. Drill him that way for several sessions, and you'll be amazed at how much he will improve. In doing this, you're re-establishing the casting concept by re-conditioning him.

Visual Aid Baseball with All Eight Casts

Description

This is the above trial-and-success visual aid baseball drill, but with four angled casts added.

Purpose of Drill

If you wish to train your dog in the four angled casts—left-angled *Back*, right-angled *Back*, left-angled *Come-in*, and right-angled *Come-*

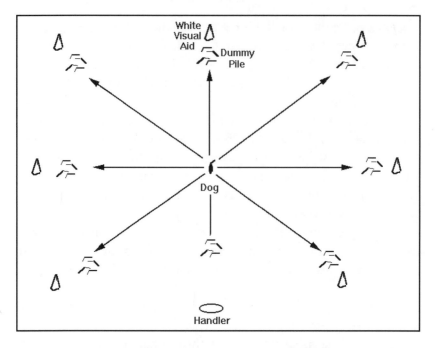

Figure 17. Visual Aid Baseball with Angled Casts.

in—you can use this drill to do so, but only after your dog already knows the four basic casts.

Prerequisites

Your dog should have completed his bare-ground training in the four basic casts with the above visual aid casting drill.

Equipment and Facilities

You need four additional visual aids (for a total of seven or eight, depending on whether you use one for the bunt position). You need enough dummies for eight dummy piles. With six dummies at each station, the total number needed is four dozen! (You can get by with fewer by replenishing each station frequently.) Ideally, you should have some combination of eight different kinds and colors of dummies, so you can put a different kind or color at each station. That will help you keep track of how many dummies remain at each station.

Precautions and Pitfalls

Avoid sending your dog to a station that no longer has any

dummies. Put out a fixed number (three to six) of dummies of a different kind or color at each station. As your dog retrieves dummies to you, toss each kind or color into a separate pile behind you. Then a glance at these piles will tell you which stations still have dummies.

Don't overwork your dog in any one session. Eight stations call for a lot of casts, so watch your dog to see if he is either too tired or too bored.

Process—Steps in Training

After you have taken your dog through the bare-ground phase of the above visual aid baseball with the four basic casts, introduce each of the angled casts individually, as you did the basic four casts. Then pair them up, and finally use all eight stations simultaneously. Cast him to each station with the visual aids in place a couple of times. Then repeat with them removed. Add length to the casts.

After your dog can handle this on bare ground, go to cover. Shorten up. Cast him to each station with the visual aids in place a couple of times. Then repeat with them removed.

Addenda

As indicated in Chapter 7, angled casts are high-risk handling techniques that truly benefit only those involved in competitive field trials. In hunting and noncompetitive hunt tests, they seldom offer any advantage commensurate with the associated risk of refusals. As also indicated in Chapter 7, retrievers trained in the basic four casts will take angled casts reasonably well with no additional training.

Visual Aid Baseball In Water

Description

In this aquatic version of the trial-and-success visual aid baseball drill, most of the infield is in a small oval pond. First and third bases are at opposite ends of the pond. Home plate is on shore halfway between them. Second base is about 20 yards up on shore opposite home plate. And the pitcher's mound is smack in the middle of the pond!

Obviously, the trainer can't heel his dog from the plate to the mound before each cast, so he does the next best thing. He heels him around the pond and leaves him sitting on the far shore on a line

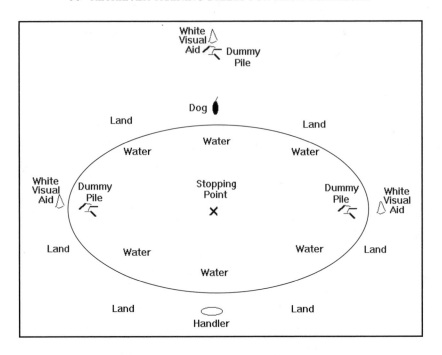

Figure 18. Visual Aid Casting Drill in Water.

between home plate and second base. Then, after huffing and puffing back around the pond to home plate, the trainer toots the *Come-in* whistle to call his dog into the water and onto the mound. When he gets there, the trainer blows the *Stop*-whistle and gives his dog an *Over* or a *Back* cast. After the dog delivers the dummy, the trainer heels him back around the pond, leaves him there, returns to home plate, and so on.

Purpose of Drill

This drill introduces your dog to both stopping and casting in water, with no risk of a popping problem. Were you to line your dog from home plate toward second base, then stop him in the middle of the pond to cast him, you would create a popping problem, which you could overcome only with the e-collar. (In fact, D. L. Walters showed me this drill in the mid-1970s specifically to help me through a popping problem. I've used it ever since to avoid popping.)

Prerequisites

Your dog should be advanced in visual aid baseball on land and should stop reliably on the whistle. He should, of course, understand the significance of visual aids.

Equipment and Facilities

You need three visual aids and enough dummies for three dummy piles. Here, too, you should put a different color of dummy at each station to help you keep track of how many dummies are left at each station.

You need a relatively small oval pond, one you can walk around rather quickly.

Precautions and Pitfalls

Don't cast your dog to a station devoid of dummies. Use three different colors of dummies, and put a fixed number (three or four) of a specific color at each base. As your dog delivers each dummy to you, toss it onto a pile of similarly colored dummies behind you. Before casting him, glance at the dummy piles behind you to see whether the bases are still "loaded."

Since you heel your dog around the pond and then walk back before each cast, you won't often overwork your dog in this drill. Nevertheless, watch him for signs of tiring.

Process—Steps in Training

With your "playing field" set up as shown in the diagram, heel your dog to the far side of the pond, leave him sitting there, and return to home plate.

(*Nota bene*: Initially you should "pattern" your dog to jump in the pond and swim straight at you when you blow the *Come-in* whistle. Otherwise, he may follow your example—you just walked around the pond—and run the bank instead. To pattern him, first toss a dummy to the middle of the pond, near the pitcher's mound, and then toot the *Come-in* whistle. Then he'll jump into the pond rather than run around it. After patterning him this way once, you shouldn't have to do it again.)

After his patterning retrieve, heel your dog back around the pond, leave him sitting there again, and return to home plate. Toot the *Come-in* whistle. When he reaches the pitcher's mound in the middle of the pond, blow the *Stop*-whistle, and cast him to whichever base you prefer. Cast him quickly, for he can't remain in one place long while swimming. (After picking up the dummy, he may cheat the water while returning to you. If he does, and if you've been correcting him with the e-collar for such transgressions, by all means do so here.) After he delivers, heel him back around the pond and repeat the process again and again until you've cast him to all three bases however many times you feel necessary.

Addenda

Back in the mid-1970s, immediately after D. L. had taught me this drill, I used it regularly for my Golden, Brandy, in an ideal little pond near my home. However, to heel Brandy around the pond, I had to follow a narrow, weed-covered dike, part of which was slightly under water. A huge (nonpoisonous) water snake lived thereabouts. Now and then, on our first trip in a session, we startled this snake as it slumbered there. As it departed—and it always waited until we were almost stepping on it—it created a small tidal wave, with appropriate sound effects. Brandy didn't mind, but I about had a heart attack—every time. This happened several times that summer and, being more than a little absent-minded, I was taken by surprise every time.

Two-Dummy Baseball

Description

This is primarily a trial-and-success drill, but with a little trial-and-error built in. With the dog on the mound, the trainer stands at home plate and tosses two dummies, one at a time, to two different stations. Then he casts his dog to the dummy he threw first. When the dog delivers it, the trainer heels him back to the mound, leaves him sitting there, returns to home plate and tosses the dummy to another station. Then he casts the dog to the *other* dummy, the one he had thrown earlier. Thereafter, he tosses each delivered dummy to a different station and casts the dog, not to it, but to the other, previously thrown dummy. He never casts the dog for the most recently thrown dummy.

Purpose of Drill

With this drill, you can introduce your dog to all four casts (or all eight, if you intend to teach him angled casts) with a minimum of equipment. You can also use it to prepare your dog for walking baseball (below).

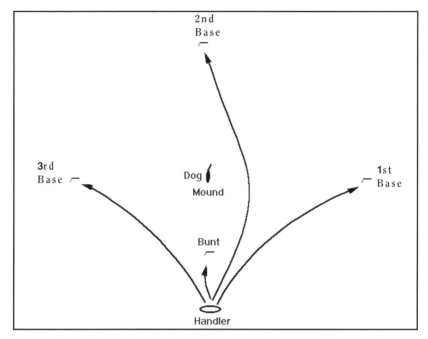

Figure 19. Two-Dummy Baseball.

Prerequisites

Your dog should be well started in lining, and should be steady enough to sit still at a distance while you toss dummies.

Equipment and Facilities

You need only two dark dummies, preferably small plastic knobbies (which you can throw quite a distance), and a flat, bare-ground or closely clipped area of reasonable size.

Precautions and Pitfalls

Since the length of the casts you can give is determined by how far you can throw the dummy from home plate—which isn't very far—this drill should be limited to introductory work only, lest your dog never learn to carry your casts a reasonable distance.

Don't overwork your dog in any one session.

Process—Steps in Training

Set up your imaginary baseball diamond in a flat, bare-ground or closely clipped area. Leave your dog sitting on the mound and walk to home plate. If your dog doesn't yet know the casts, start out with one dummy. Toss it to second base and cast your dog *Back*. Repeat this several times, perhaps for two or three sessions, until he is comfortable with the *Back* cast. Next, teach him the opposite cast, the *Come-in*. With him on the mound and you at home plate, toss a dummy to land between you, and give him a *Come-in* cast. Ditto for the two *Over* casts.

When your dog is comfortable with all four casts individually, combine them into pairs of opposites. With him sitting on the mound and you standing at home plate, toss the first dummy to second base and the other one to the bunt position. Now cast him to second base. If he tries to come in for the bunt dummy, proceed as follows: Rush toward him, repeating the *Back* cast encouragingly; then, after he delivers the second base dummy, pick up the other dummy and start over.

As soon as he takes your *Back* cast properly, he's ready to move on. When he delivers the dummy from second base, heel him back to the mound, and return to home plate. Toss the dummy back to second base. Now give him a *Come-in* cast to the bunt dummy, the one that has been on the ground longer. If he starts to go back, proceed as follows: Holler "No! No! No!" and toot the *Come-in* whistle as often as necessary to bring him back; then, after he delivers the bunt position dummy, walk out and pick up the second base dummy, and start over; toss the bunt dummy first, then the second base dummy; and again give him a *Come-in* cast. Continue working on these two casts this way until he consistently takes both casts properly.

Next, repeat the process with the two *Over* casts. Toss the first dummy to, say, first base and the second dummy to third base. Then cast him to first base. And so on until he can handle both of these as a pair.

Thereafter, you can toss the dummies to any two of the stations in any sequence you like. Always cast your dog to the one that has been on the ground longer. When he delivers it, toss it to another station, and cast him for the other dummy. And so on.

Addenda

If you can find just the right type of pond or lake, you can use this drill in water, too. You need to be able to put your dog on the end of a point, with water on three sides of him. You also need calm water, so the dummies won't drift too much.

As mentioned above, you can use this drill to prepare your dog for walking baseball (below).

D. L.'s Walking Baseball

Description

Pro D. L. Walters developed this highly productive trial-and-success "polishing" drill many years ago. It has been one of my favorites ever since D. L. showed it to me in the mid-1970s. It's easy to do. It takes very little time. It requires minimal equipment (two red plastic dummies), and only the most ordinary bare-ground field. Then, too, in addition to sharpening up the dog's casting, it even, as a fringe benefit, helps his marking!

If you were to watch someone doing this drill, you would think it a totally random sequence of events. The handler and dog are in a park or school-yard. The dog retrieves a dummy to the handler, who tosses it off in some direction. Then the handler leaves the dog sitting there and walks away. When he stops, he gives the dog a cast—but not to the dummy he just threw! The dog takes the cast and, wonder of wonders, finds another dummy. After he delivers it, the handler tosses it off somewhere else, and again walks away from the dog. He stops and gives the dog another cast, this time to the first dummy you saw him throw, not

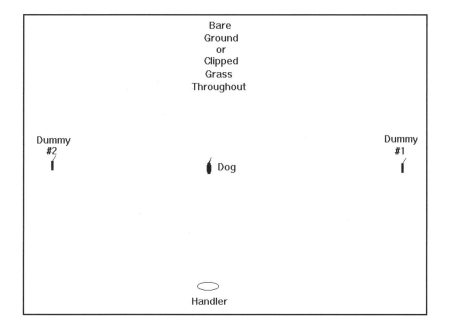

Figure 20. D. L. Walters' Walking Baseball, First Station.

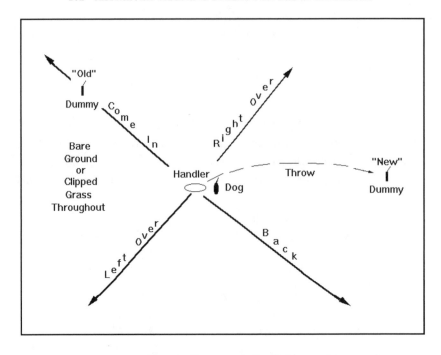

Figure 21. D. L. Walters' Walking Baseball, All "Floating" Diamonds.

this more recent one. And, by golly, the dog takes the cast and finds that dummy. And so it goes. If you are quite observant, you would notice that the handler mixes up his casts—left-*Over, Back, Come-in,* right-*Over*—more or less randomly. And, every time, he sends the dog to the dummy that has been on the ground longer. Amazing.

If the handler were quite skilled, you would notice that at the end of about a ten-minute session, in which he gave his dog a couple of each cast, he ends up right where he had started out, near his vehicle. He made a big, zig-zaggy loop.

Clearly, this drill has a lot more discipline, a lot more order, than casual observation would reveal. The handler mixed up his casts nicely. He always sent his dog for the "older" dummy. They ended up about where they started out. And yet they seemed to wander aimlessly all over the park. Hmmmm.

Purpose of Drill

This is a "polishing" drill, not a teaching drill. You use it only after your dog knows his casts very well. Done regularly, it keeps him very sharp. If his responses to some cast become sloppy in real blind retrieves, this drill—with emphasis on the weak cast—will correct the problem.

Although not suitable in cover, you can use this drill to introduce all manner of terrain problems into your casting drills, provided you can find them in bare ground or closely clipped areas.

This drill is highly "productive," in that it makes excellent use of training time. The only "slack" time between casts is spent by the handler walking from one station to the next. Another dimension of its productivity is that it seems to help the dog's marking. The dog has to mark and remember both dummies, which strengthens his overall marking ability.

Prerequisites

Your dog should be proficient in all his casts. It's most helpful, although not absolutely necessary, if he has gone through the above two-dummy baseball drill, which accustoms a dog to being cast to the dummy that has been on the ground longer.

Equipment and Facilities

You need only two red dummies, preferably plastic knobbies, which you can throw quite a distance. Red dummies are ideal because you can see them so well, but your dog (being color-blind) won't see them until he is very close to them. If the grass in your bare-ground area is a tad high, you should use large dummies, so you will be able to see both dummies all the time. If the grass is short or nonexistent, use small dummies, because they will be adequately visible to you.

You need a bare-ground area large enough to allow you to wander around as you do this drill. A park or school-yard would be ideal. Initially, a flat area is best, but later on, rolling ground will add challenges.

Precautions and Pitfalls

Don't try this drill in cover. To make it work, you must be able to see the dummies all the time. If you can't, this drill degenerates into a debacle, in which neither you nor your dog has the foggiest notion where either bloomin' dummy might be.

Initially, keep the casts relatively short, so your dog will find the dummy quickly. Later, after he understands walking baseball, you can lengthen his casts out to whatever distance you like. But if you make them too long too soon, he will fail often and become quite confused. You want him to enjoy this drill, so he must experience success, especially at first.

Don't overwork your dog in any one session. Because this drill is so productive, time-wise, you may be tempted to overwork your dog while doing it. You may find it difficult to quit after eight or ten casts, which take only ten or twelve minutes. Remember: Your dog gets much more exercise than you do during that brief period.

Process—Steps in Training

Think of this drill as Nathan Detroit's floating crap-game in the musical, *Guys and Dolls*. The crap-game was always the same, but the location kept changing. In that sense, walking baseball is a floating baseball game. Each time your dog delivers a dummy to you, you leave him sitting there for his next cast. Thus, each "delivery point" becomes a new pitcher's mound. Then, you walk to a new place from which to cast him, thereby establishing a new home plate. Of course, when your dog delivers the dummy to you at that home plate, you leave him sitting there, which converts it into the next pitcher's mound. And so on. In walking baseball, the entire baseball diamond moves from place to place. The location and layout of each new diamond depends entirely on where the handler establishes his next home plate. (Similarly, in *Guys and Dolls*, the location and layout of the floating crap-game depended entirely on where Nathan Detroit felt the game would be safest from Lieutenant Brannigan's vigilance.) The entire diamond "floats"—but the casting game remains the same.

But, of course, before you can float the diamond, you must start it somewhere. Since this fixed starting point diamond differs from all the subsequent floating diamonds, it is diagrammed separately. The subsequent floating diamonds are identical, in that they offer the same range of options, so one diagram suffices for all of them.

To Start the Session: Have your dog sit anywhere in your (bare-ground) training area. Toss one dummy to his left and the other to his right, about twenty yards each. Now walk straight away from your dog for perhaps twenty yards. Turn and give him an *Over* to the *first* dummy you tossed. That's all there is to the first station.

To Float the Subsequent Diamonds: When your dog delivers the dummy to you, have him sit. Toss the dummy he just delivered at an angle of about 120 degrees from the spot where the other dummy lies.

Where your dog is now sitting becomes the first of a series of floating pitcher's mounds. After you leave him and establish a new home plate, you'll cast him, not to the dummy you just threw, but to the other one, the second one you threw at the starting diamond.

But before you leave your dog, you must decide in which direction you should walk and how far. You choose the direction based on the cast you want to give him next. If you decide to give him a *Back*, you'll walk straight away from your dog on the line that extends from him to the intended dummy. If you decide to give him a *Come-in*, you'll walk from your dog toward and then past that dummy. If you decide to give him an *Over*, you'll walk away at a 90-degree angle, one way or the other, to the line from your dog to the dummy.

So much for which direction. To determine how far to walk, you must decide how long a cast you want your dog to take, not on this cast, but on the next one. Wherever you stop will become the dog's next mound, for he'll deliver to you there. You'll cast him from that next mound to the dummy you just threw before leaving him this time. So, this time you should walk far enough to reach a point that will make his next cast as long or short as you want.

Until you and your retriever have played walking baseball a few times, you may find this drill a little confusing. So, to help you through that period, here are four basic rules to fall back on whenever you're uncertain about what you should do next.

1. Always toss the delivered dummy at a reasonable angle from the other dummy, the one already on the ground. Initially, make the angle at least 120 degrees. Later, after your dog understands this drill, you can reduce it to 90 degrees.

2. Never cast your dog to the dummy you most recently threw. Always send him for the one that has been on the ground longer.

3. When walking away from your dog, choose the direction that allows you to give him the cast you want to give him this time.

4. When walking away from your dog, walk far enough from the dummy you most recently threw to make your *next cast* the length you want it to be. Wherever you stop will become home plate for this cast and therefore the pitcher's mound for the next.

As you can see, you can mix up your casts at will, and you can make each cast precisely as long as you want it to be. You establish which cast you'll give *this time* by the direction in which you walk when you leave your dog. You determine how long his *next* cast, not this one, will be by how far you walk. These two options—the direction and distance you walk—give this drill amazing flexibility, and therefore, productivity.

Thus, you move from place to place as you give your dog whatever sequence of casts you choose. Normally, in about ten minutes, you can give him two of each cast, and long casts at that.

But how in the world can you end this drill without violating Rule #2? Rule #2 says you should never cast your dog for the dummy you most recently threw. So, when you decide to end the session, how do you pick up the last dummy, the one still on the ground? After all, at that point, it *is* the one you most recently threw.

"Elementary, my dear Watson!" Instead of casting your dog, you should line him to it! *Touché!*

Addenda

If you can find bare-ground or closely clipped areas with rolling ground, you can work your dog through all manner of terrain hazards with this drill.

The recommendation that you throw each dummy at an angle of about 120 degrees away from the other dummy is a good initial rule. It keeps the two dummies widely separated both physically and in the dog's memory. But, as mentioned above, after your dog is comfortable with walking baseball, you can tighten that angle a bit. However, don't slice it any finer than 90 degrees. You don't want your dog to scent the wrong dummy after taking the cast you gave him. If he does, he'll veer off for it, and who can blame him?

After you have played walking baseball awhile, you'll be able to lay out a plan for each session that will allow you to end up back where you started, near your vehicle. That will make your sessions even shorter, for you will waste no time getting back to the car after you finish all the casts you want to give the dog. Of course, don't worry about optimizing your route around the course until you and your dog are quite comfortable with the drill itself.

9
Combination
Drills

This chapter contains six drills that combine two or three of the parts of the blind retrieve. Two drills (inverted double-T and swim-by) combine stopping and casting. Three drills (double-T, anti-scalloping, and do-all) combine lining, stopping, and casting. One drill (casting into water) can be set up two ways; in one it combines just stopping and casting; in the other, it combines lining, stopping, and casting. You should delay using these drills until your dog has mastered each of the three parts of the blind retrieve individually through the separate drills (Chapters 4 through 8). The dog that doesn't line well in separate lining drills won't improve his lining in combination drills. In fact, he'll regress. Ditto for stopping and casting.

These combination drills have three functions. First, they advance your dog a long ways toward real blinds. Even though he can do each part of the blind retrieve individually, in his canine mind they are just three independent functions. By linking them up in these combination drills, you lead him into grasping the connection between them. Second, some of these drills facilitate introducing various land and water hazards into your dog's blind retrieves. You can set them up so that, in both lining and casting, he must either drive through obstacles (like a patch of heavy cover) or ignore attractions (like decoys). Third, you can use these drills all through your dog's active life to work out the predictable problems he will develop as he runs more and more real blind retrieves. For example, at some point, he will begin to scallop *Back* on his *Over* casts. Or, as he develops more confidence in his own ability, he may start turning you off—slipping whistles and refusing your casts. And so on. As these problems come up, you can put them to rest, at least

temporarily, by giving him a refresher course in the appropriate combination drills.

NOTES

The following two *Notes* are referenced in several of the drills.

Note on Identifying the Dummy Piles

In general, you can identify dummy piles for your dog in any one
of the following three ways:

1. You can use visual aids for each pile until you've run your dog to
   each one once or twice. Then you should remove the visual aids
   and run the drill without them. If you use the same location for a
   given drill through several sessions, you shouldn't need the visual
   aids after the first session.

2. You can have an assistant "mark the piles" before you start the
   drill. To do this, he should walk out, toss a dummy to the pile while
   your dog watches, and then get out of sight. This technique is also
   used in the modern sight blind drill in Chapter 4. When using it
   here, your assistant should mark one pile, then you should handle
   (line or cast) your dog to that pile at least twice before repeating
   the process at the next pile. And so on.

3. If you have no assistant, you can walk out and mark the pile yourself, then walk back and handle your dog to it. This is time consuming, especially in water work, which requires that you walk
   around the lake. Frankly, when you're training alone, visual aids
   are better.

Note on Stocking the Dummy Piles

As has been previously pointed out, in any drill with multiple
dummy piles, you need a method of keeping track of how many dummies remain in each pile. If you send your dog to an empty pile, you confuse him and upset the flow of the training session. To avoid this minor
disaster, put a fixed number of dummies of a specific color or kind in
each pile. For example, if you are using three dummy piles, you might
put six red ones in the first pile, six black ones in the second, and six gray

ones in the third. Then, as your dog delivers each dummy to you, toss it into a pile of like dummies behind you. As the drill progresses, you will build three piles behind you, one for red dummies, one for black, and one for gray. When any pile behind you has six dummies, you know the corresponding dummy pile is empty.

To make this work, you should put the same number of dummies in each pile. When working your dog, you have too much to think about without having to remember that you put, say, four dummies in one pile, seven in another, and nine in a yet another. When you're working only one dog, six is a nice number of dummies for each pile.

If, in a given drill, you have to put out more dummy piles than you have different colors of dummies, use different sizes or types as well as different colors. Perhaps you put out eighteen small plastic knobbies (six reds, six blacks, and six grays), and still have three more piles to stock. Use eighteen large plastic knobbies (red, black, and white). Or use three different kinds or sizes of canvas dummies.

DRILLS

Inverted Double-T

Description

As the diagram shows, the layout for this trial-and-success drill looks like a "T" that has been crossed twice in the middle instead of once at the top. The T's upright should be at least 100 yards long. The two crossbars should cut the upright into three approximately equal segments. Each crossbar should be at least 60 yards long. With such a layout, the trainer can give his dog *Over* casts of 30 yards, *Back* casts of about 35 and 70 yards, and *Come-in* casts of about 15, 50, and 85 yards. As the diagram shows, there are six dummy piles, one at the top of the upright leg, one at each end of both crossbars, and one about halfway between the base of the upright and the intersection of the first crossbar leg.

This is called the "inverted" double-T because the trainer runs it backwards from the regular double-T (below). In the latter, he would line his dog from the base of the T toward the other end, and then stop and cast him when he reaches one or the other crossbars. In this inverted version, instead of lining his dog, the trainer heels him to the far end of

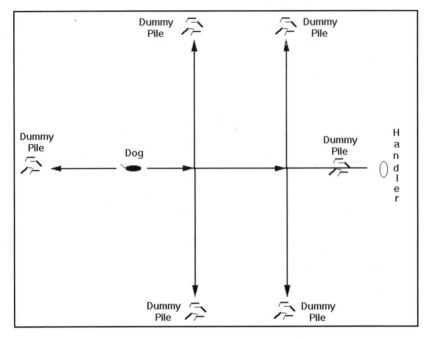

Figure 22. Inverted Double-T.

the T, leaves him there in a *Sit-Stay*, returns to the base of the T, and handles him from there. First, he toots the *Come-in* whistle. When the dog reaches the intersection of either crossbar, the trainer stops him with the *Sit*-whistle. Then, he can give him any of the four regular casts.

Because the trainer doesn't repeatedly line and stop his dog, as he would in the regular double-T, he won't create a popping problem. Thus, for those who would rather avoid popping than cure it, the inverted version is ideal.

However, in the inverted double-T, the trainer must spend a lot of time walking back and forth on the T's upright, as he heels his dog to the far end and then returns to the base. Pros with big strings of dogs can't afford to waste so much time walking each one back and forth repeatedly, so they rely on the regular double-T and cure popping with the e-collar. However, the inverted version should better serve the needs of amateurs with only one or two dogs.

Purpose of Drill

This drill allows you to drill your dog in both stopping and casting with zero risk of creating a popping problem.

Prerequisites

The dog should know the four basic casts and should stop on the whistle reliably.

Equipment and Facilities

You need enough dummies for six dummy piles. To initially identify the piles for your dog, you need either visual aids or an assistant.

Initially, you need a flat, bare-ground or closely clipped field of appropriate size (at least 100 yards by 60 yards). Later, after your dog is familiar with this drill, you may want to set it up in a place with terrain and cover hazards.

Precautions and Pitfalls

Avoid sending your dog to an empty dummy pile. (See *Note on Stocking Dummy Piles*, above.)

Don't slip into the habit of always stopping your dog at the same crossbar. The primary purpose of having two crossbars is to keep him from always stopping in the same place. So mix them up in random sequence. Also, you should now and then give him a *Come-in* cast all the way from the far end of the T to the *Come-in* dummy pile near the line. That way, he won't stop at either crossbar.

Because you must heel your dog 100 yards and then walk back that same 100 yards before each cast, you won't normally overwork him in any one session—but it's still possible. So watch how he's holding up.

Process—Steps in Training

Start out with a single-T layout, that is, a T with only one crossbar (either one). Make sure your dog knows where all the dummy piles are located. (See *Note on Identifying the Dummy Piles*, above.) Heel your dog to the top of the T, leave him sitting there, return to the line (base of T), and toot the *Come-in* whistle. When he reaches the crossbar, blow the *Stop*-whistle. Give him any of the four basic casts. Repeat this a couple of times for each cast. Stay with the Single-T in the same location until you feel he has mastered it, which may take two or three sessions.

After he understands the Single-T, continue using the same location but add the second crossbar, and introduce your dog to the two new dummy piles. Then work him on the full drill.

Addenda

After your dog is familiar with this setup, you can use it in cover, too, as long as you always start out identifying the dummy piles for your dog.

Double-T

Description

This mostly trial-and-success drill combines lining, stopping, and casting. It has been around at least since the early 1960s, and probably longer. Like the inverted double-T, above, it is run on a flat, bare-ground field of appropriate size (at least 100 yards by 60 yards). The double-T pattern differs only slightly from that of the inverted double-T. It, too, should have an upright at least 100 yards long with two intersecting crossbars at least 60 yards long. However, since a person shouldn't stop his dog too soon after sending him on a line, the first crossbar is usually at least 50 yards from the base of T. The other crossbar is usually about halfway between the first crossbar and the top of the T. Dummy piles are

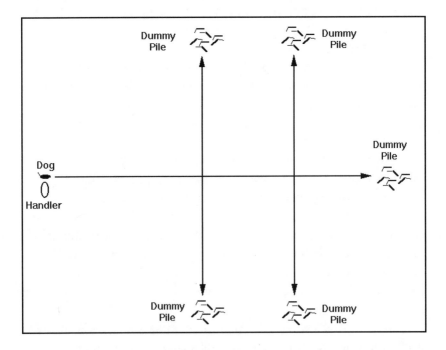

Figure 23. Double-T.

placed at the top of the T and at both ends of each crossbar. However, unlike the inverted double-T, there is no *Come-in* dummy pile between the line and the intersection of the first crossbar. Dummies there would interfere with lining the dog up the T. To give his dog a *Come-in* cast, the trainer surreptitiously tosses a dummy to that spot after his dog has run past it in lining.

In the double-T drill, the trainer lines his dog up the upright of the T, sometimes letting him go all the way to the end, other times stopping him at either of the crossbars and casting him left, right, or back.

The double-T can be run on land, in water, or in any combination of the two. The ideal water situation would be a pond about 100 yards long and 60 yards wide.

Purpose of Drill

This drill allows you to combine the three parts of the blind retrieve into a single drill. In doing this, you advance an inexperienced dog from the individual drills for lining, stopping, and casting into more demanding drills, as you prepare him for real blind retrieves. You can also use this drill to correct bad habits that crop up through your dog's active life, like sloppy casts and whistle refusals.

Prerequisites

The dog should be well advanced in the individual lining, stopping, and casting drills. Since this drill encourages popping, he should have been e-collar-conditioned.

Equipment and Facilities

You need enough dummies for five dummy piles. To initially identify the piles for your dog, you need either visual aids or an assistant. Because of the popping problem, you need an e-collar, preferably with continuous stimulation.

For land work, you need a flat, bare-ground or closely clipped field at least 100 yards by 60 yards. For water work, you need a pond of similar dimensions.

Precautions and Pitfalls

This drill will absolutely, positively create a popping problem, which you will have to correct with the e-collar. If you are unwilling to use an e-collar on your dog, don't use this drill!

Avoid sending your dog to an empty dummy pile. (See *Note on Stocking the Dummy Piles,* above.)

Since you have so many casting options, you should be especially careful not to overwork your dog in any one session. Remember: Every time you say *Back!* he runs at least 160 yards, and usually 200-plus yards.

Process—Steps in Training

Start out with a single-T, using either of the crossbars. Make sure your dog knows where all the dummy piles are. (See *Note on Identifying the Dummy Piles*, above.) Line him up the upright of the T. For the first several times, let him go all the way and pick up a dummy at the top of the T. Thereafter, occasionally stop him at the upright, and give him any of the basic casts. Throughout this drill, to minimize the popping problem, let him go all the way more often than you stop him.

After he is comfortable with the single-T, add the second crossbar. Again, make sure he knows where all the dummy piles are. Now work your dog into the full drill, using both crossbars. For the *Come-in* cast, do this: Line him toward the far end of the T; while he's still highballing for the far end, toss a dummy between you and the first intersection. Then stop him and give him a *Come-in* cast to the dummy you just tossed.

Addenda

Don't overdo this drill. Some amateurs seem to run the double-T whenever they can't think of anything else to do! If your dog needs work on lining, better drills are available for just lining. Ditto for casting. However, if he needs work on stopping—if he's been slipping whistles on real blinds—this drill will help. Still, you'll accomplish more by strapping the e-collar around his neck and running some real blinds. Whenever he slips a whistle, use the transmitter button to *'splain it to 'im so's he can understand it!*

Anti-Scalloping Drill

Description

As a retriever gains experience in real blind retrieves, he begins to scallop *Back* when given an *Over* cast. Why? Because, in the "real

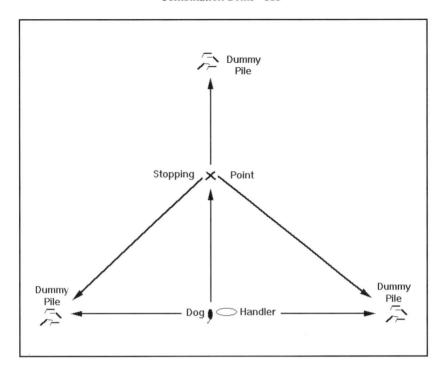

Figure 24. Anti-Scalloping Drill.

world," 80-plus percent of the casts most dogs receive are angled *Back*s. This may make sense in the fiercely competitive field trial environment, but it must be called "unfortunate" throughout the rest of retrieverdom. Then, too, most trainers concentrate on long blinds, so the dogs come to expect long blinds. When stopped short of normal length, they know they "jest ain't out there far enough yet." So they scallop *Back* on *Over* casts.

Years ago, pro D. L. Walters showed me a trial-and-success drill to counteract this scalloping tendency. He uses a three-legged pattern blind, with each leg about 100 yards long, and separated by 90-degree angles. As the diagram shows, the two outside legs form a straight line 200 yards long. The middle leg runs perpendicular from the center of that straight line. With this setup, D. L. lines the dog to all three dummy piles a couple of times. Then he lines him toward the middle pile, and stops him about 60 yards out. He casts the dog *Over* to one or the other of the outside dummy piles. In taking this cast, the dog must angle *in* toward the known dummy pile. With enough repetitions over a reasonable period of time, this inward momentum overcomes the dog's tendency to scallop back.

Purpose of Drill

This drill combines lining, stopping, and casting into one drill. It also counteracts any tendency the dog may have to scallop *Back* on *Over* casts. It works most effectively as a preventative, that is, by accustoming the dog to this drill before he begins to scallop. It also works as a cure for the dog that has started scalloping before being introduced to this drill. Finally, it conditions the dog to run long *Over* casts.

Prerequisites

The dog should be well along in lining, stopping, and casting. He should be accustomed to running multi-spoke pattern blinds (see Chapter 10). Since this drill encourages popping, the dog should have been e-collar-conditioned.

Equipment and Facilities

You need enough dummies for three dummy piles. To initially identify the piles for your dog, you need either visual aids or an assistant. Since this drill encourages popping, you need an e-collar, preferably with continuous stimulation.

You need a flat field about 200 yards by 100 yards, either bare ground or with light cover.

Precautions and Pitfalls

As mentioned above, this drill encourages popping, so be prepared to make appropriate e-collar corrections.

Avoid sending your dog to an empty dummy pile. (See *Note on Stocking the Dummy Piles*, above.)

Your dog runs a long way every time you say *Back*, so be careful not to overwork him in any one session.

Process—Steps in Training

Lay out the three legs as shown in the diagram. Make sure your dog knows where the dummy piles are. (See *Note on Identifying the Dummy Piles*, above.) With that done, you can run the full drill. Line him to the middle pile. Sometimes let him go all the way and pick up a dummy there. Sometimes stop him at about 60 yards and cast him left-*Over*, right-*Over*, and at least occasionally *Back*.

Addenda

Scalloping *Back* can become a serious problem as a retriever gains experience in real blind retrieves. Thus, this drill is highly useful. If you prefer not to use the e-collar, you could run it "backwards," like the inverted double-T.

Do-All Drill

Description

The diagram of this trial-and-error drill looks like a backlash on a bait-casting reel! I have included it, not to recommend it, but just to show you how complex these combination drills can become. Laid out as

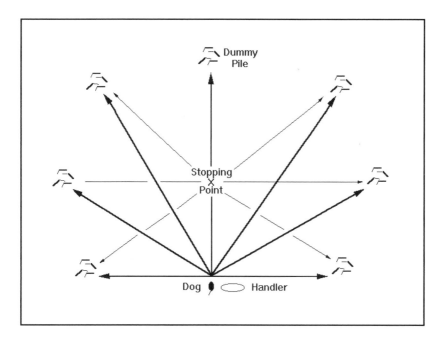

Figure 25. "Do-All" Combination Drill.

in the diagram, this is a seven-legged lining and casting pattern field that allows the trainer line his dog to seven different dummy piles and to cast him (from the stopping point in the middle) in all eight directions. He can line him straight to each pile. In casting, he lines the dog up the middle leg, stops him, then casts him to whichever dummy pile he chooses.

Incidentally, this drill can be run on land, in water, or in any combination of the two.

Purpose of Drill

This drill gives the thoroughly trained retriever a refresher course in multi-spoke lining drills and in all eight casts.

Prerequisites

The dog should be fully trained and should have had extensive experience with real blind retrieves. He should have been e-collar-conditioned.

Equipment and Facilities

You need enough dummies for seven dummy piles. To initially identify the piles for your dog, you need either visual aids or an assistant. You need an e-collar to keep your dog on the path of truth and virtue through this maze of lining and casting possibilities. (If, in a maze like this, you get lost as easily as I do, you probably need a map of the area, a compass, some flares, and perhaps a cell-phone on which to call 911!)

You need a suitable field, large enough to allow the length of lines and casts you want, and having whatever terrain and cover hazards you want to work into the drill. If you plan to run this drill in water, you need a fairly large pond or a lake, again with whatever hazards you would like to include.

Precautions and Pitfalls

Like all drills that combine lining and stopping, this drill encourages popping. However, most trainers who use it have already taken the pop out of their dogs with the e-collar.

Avoid sending your dog to an empty dummy pile. (See *Note on Stocking the Dummy Piles*, above.)

Do not overwork your dog in any one session. It would be impossible to run him on all options of this drill in one session without overworking him!

Process—Steps in Training

If you are so disposed, set this monster up wherever you can, and make sure your dog knows where all the dummy piles are—if he can count that high! (See *Note on Identifying the Dummy Piles*, above.) Line him to each pile. After he knows his way to the end of each of the seven spokes, begin the combination lining and casting drill. Always line him up the middle spoke. Sometimes let him go all the way and pick up a dummy at the far end. Other times, stop him at the designated place and, from the mind-boggling array of available options, choose one cast and give it to him. And so on.

Addenda

Before getting into a drill this complex, in which you will almost certainly have to correct your dog many times, ask yourself whether it has the potential to make your dog that much more useful to you. Unless you are a field trial competitor, the answer will probably be, "Really, Old Thing, you must be jesting!"

Swim-By

Description

This trial-and-error anti-bank-running drill doesn't begin until the dog re-enters the water while returning from lining to a dummy pile across the pond. Actually, a mark over there would work just as well as a blind. Either would get the dog swimming back to the trainer with a dummy in his mouth, which is the essence of this drill. When he reaches the middle of the pond, the trainer blows the *Stop*-whistle and casts him toward the end of the pond. After enough training, he will swim all the way to the end before he lands.

Purpose of Drill

This is an excellent drill for curing water cheating. If your dog will take your cast and stay in the water when he already has a dummy in his mouth and is returning to you, he'll do it anytime! It also combines stopping and casting in water in a way that precludes popping.

Prerequisites

The dog should be advanced in casting in water, and should stop reliably on the whistle. He should have been e-collar-conditioned.

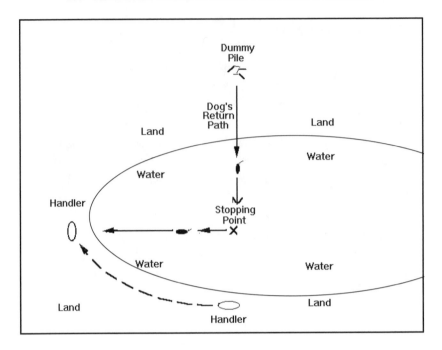

Figure 26. Swim-By.

Equipment and Facilities

You need enough dummies to set up the blind (or mark) across the pond. If you opt for a blind, you need either a visual aid or an assistant to initially identify the dummy pile for your dog. If you opt for a mark, you need either an assistant or a dummy launcher to throw the mark. You should have an e-collar, preferably with momentary stimulation.

You need a suitable body of water.

Precautions and Pitfalls

Avoid e-collar corrections while your dog is actually in the water. When he veers off toward land too soon, try to handle him back onto the right path. Only if he actually reaches shore should you nick him with the e-collar.

If you opt for a blind, avoid sending your dog to an empty dummy pile. (See *Note on Stocking the Dummy Piles*, above.)

Don't overwork your dog in any one session.

Process—Steps in Training

Set up the test according to the diagram, with either a blind or a mark across the water. (If you opt for a blind, see *Note on Identifying the Dummy Piles*, above.) On his return with the dummy, when your dog reaches the middle of the pond, blow the *Stop*-whistle and give him an *Over* toward the end of the pond. Then, immediately, hustle to the end of the pond so he'll swim straight toward you as he carries your cast.

Next time, after giving him the *Over*, move toward the end of the pond, but don't go all the way there. If he curves in toward you, say "No!" and repeat the cast. If he actually lands short of the end of the pond, nick him with the e-collar.

Continue this, but each time shorten the distance you walk. Eventually your dog will take your cast all the way to the end of the pond, even when you do not move from your original position.

Addenda

Although included here among water-casting drills, this is primarily a drill to prevent or cure water cheating in blind retrieves.

Some trainers prepare their dogs for this drill by simulating it on land, mostly during the double-T or inverted double-T drill. There, too, as the dog returns with a dummy, the trainer stops him with the *Sit*-whistle, then casts him left or right, and insists that he carry that cast until he hears the *Come-in* whistle. This preparatory step greatly simplifies teaching the swim-by in water.

Casting into Water

Description

This mostly trial-and-success drill is run along the shore of a body of water, primarily to give the trainer opportunities to cast his dog from land into water. Some dogs are reluctant to take casts from land into the water.

This drill can be run either straight or inverted. To run it straight, the trainer lines his dog toward the dummy pile on land down the shore, then stops him at the designated spot and casts him—either *Over* into the water for the dummy pile across the pond,

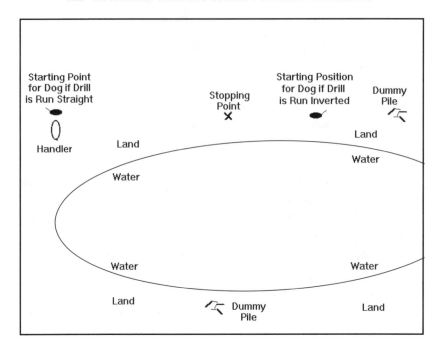

Figure 27. Casting into Water.

or *Back* to the dummy pile down the shoreline. To run it inverted, the trainer heels his dog down past the designated stopping point, leaves him sitting there, returns to the line, and toots the *Come-in* whistle. When the dog reaches the designated spot, the trainer blows the *Stop*-whistle, then casts him either *Over* into the water or *Back* down the shoreline.

Purpose of Drill
This drill accustoms the dog to take casts from land into water.

Prerequisites
The dog should be well along in lining, stopping, and casting drills. If you plan to use the straight version, which encourages popping, your dog should have been e-collar-conditioned.

Equipment and Facilities
You need enough dummies for two dummy piles. To initially identify the dummy piles for your dog, you need either visual aids or an

assistant. If you plan to run the straight version, you need an e-collar, preferably with continuous stimulation.

You need a pond or finger of a lake about 20 or 25 yards wide with a shoreline about 100 yards long.

Precautions and Pitfalls

If you run this drill straight, popping will be a problem. Frankly, no more often than you need to run it for the average dog, I would recommend you run it inverted.

Avoid sending your dog to an empty dummy pile. (See *Note on Stocking the Dummy Piles*, above.)

Don't overwork your dog in any one session.

Process—Steps in Training

Set the drill up in a suitable place. Make sure your dog knows where both dummy piles are. (See *Note on Identifying the Dummy Piles*, above.) To run the drill inverted, heel your dog down the shoreline well past the designated stopping point, leave him sitting there, and return to the line. Toot the *Come-in* whistle. When he reaches the designated stopping spot, blow the *Stop*-whistle, and cast him either *Over* into the water or *Back* to the dummy pile down the shoreline. In repetitions of the drill, give him both casts, but in no predictable sequence.

To run the drill straight, line your dog toward the dummy pile down the shoreline. Sometimes let him go all the way and get a dummy there. Other times, stop him at the designated stopping spot and cast him either *Over* to the dummy pile across the pond or *Back* to the dummy pile down the shoreline. In repetitions of the drill, give him both casts, but in no predictable sequence.

Addenda

You should do this drill infrequently, just often enough to be sure you can cast your dog into water from land. Beyond that, it's a waste of training time.

Photo courtesy Janet Yosey.

10
"Suction" Drills

To run a blind retrieve successfully, your dog must take the line you give him and carry it until he either finds a bird or hears your *Stop*-whistle. To state this more accurately, he must lock in on a distant "picture" in the direction in which you have "aimed" him and, when sent, he must drive toward that picture until he finds the bird or hears the whistle.

Unfortunately, any number of distractions can dissuade your dog, first, from forming a good picture and, second, from pursuing it—distractions such as the memory of a recent mark or of another blind, a distant shotgun blast, a person standing in plain sight, a stray white object, and so on. Until you train him otherwise, when your dog is thusly distracted, he'll run toward the distraction rather than take the line you give him. Since the distraction pulls him off-line as if by suction, he is said to "suck" to it. In doing this, he disturbs cover unnecessarily, and normally requires an inordinate amount of handling before he finally picks up the bird for which you sent him.

This chapter contains six drills with which you can train your dog to ignore these various distractions, or suction factors. Two drills (multi-legged pattern blind and wagon wheel) address suction to old blinds. Two drills (pattern blind with a white object distraction, and pattern blind with a distraction) address various visual and aural distractions. The remaining two drills (pattern blind with a mark at an angle, and pattern blind under the arc of a fall) address suction to previous marks.

HANDLING TECHNIQUES

After your dog is a thoroughly trained and long-experienced campaigner, when you set him up for a blind, he'll ignore all distractions, select a picture in the proper direction, then run straight at it. However, through his earlier years, you'll have to help him. Most of the time, you'll know ahead of time what the distraction will be in a particular test—an old fall, an old blind, or whatever. If so, set your dog up initially facing the distraction. When he locks in on it, say *No!* firmly but not too loudly. (When saying *No!* this way, don't put your left hand down by his head. Save that hand gesture for when you're confirming a correct picture with the verbal *Good!*) After *No*-ing him off of the distraction, re-heel him to face the blind, and go through your blind retrieve sequence (*Dead bird!—Good!—Back!* or whatever you use).

Occasionally, you won't know ahead of time what will distract your dog. After you've set him up facing the blind, he may lock in on some unexpected distraction—a stray white object, a jumping fish, whatever—off to either side. When this happens, re-heel him so he faces that distraction and say *No!* Then re-heel him to face the blind, and go through your blind retrieve sequence.

After you have taken your dog through the drills in this chapter, he'll understand what *No!* means in this context. And he will respond properly. He'll know what it means because, during these drills, you'll be *No*-ing him off of various (planned) distractions. He'll respond properly because by then he'll have experienced the unpleasant consequences of taking your *No!* too lightly. In other words, these are mostly trial-and-error drills. With the previous trial-and-success drills, you've taught your dog how pleasant life can be when he takes your line. Now, it's time to teach him how difficult life can be when he doesn't.

Nota bene: Whenever in the text, I tell you to *No* your dog off of the distraction, I mean that you should set him up facing it, say *No!* and then re-heel him facing the blind and go through your blind retrieve sequence.

NOTES

The following *Notes* are referenced in several of the drills.

Note on Identifying the Dummy Piles

In general, you can identify dummy piles for your dog in any one of the following three ways:

1. You can use visual aids for each pile until you've run your dog to each one once or twice. Then you should remove the visual aids and run the drill without them. If you use the same location for a given drill through several sessions, you shouldn't need the visual aids after the first session.

2. You can have an assistant "mark the piles" before you start the drill. To do this, he should walk out, toss a dummy to the pile while your dog watches, and then get out of sight. This technique is also used in the modern sight blind drill in Chapter 4.

3. If you have no assistant, you can walk out and mark the pile yourself, then walk back and handle your dog to it. This is time consuming, especially in water work, which requires that you walk around the lake. Frankly, when you're training alone, visual aids are better.

Note on Stocking the Dummy Piles

As has been previously pointed out, in any drill with multiple dummy piles, you need a method of keeping track of how many dummies remain in each pile. If you send your dog to an empty pile, you confuse him and upset the flow of the training session. To avoid this minor disaster, put a fixed number of dummies of a specific color or kind in each pile. For example, if you are using three dummy piles, you might put six red ones in the first pile, six black ones in the second, and six gray ones in the third. Then, as your dog delivers each dummy to you, toss it into a pile of like dummies behind you. As the drill progresses, you will build three piles behind you, one for red dummies, one for black, and one for gray. When any pile behind you has six dummies, you know the corresponding dummy pile is empty.

To make this work, you should put the same number of dummies in each pile. When working your dog, you have too much to think about without having to remember that you put, say, four dummies in one pile, seven in another, and nine in a yet another. When you're working only one dog, six is a nice number of dummies for each pile.

If, in a given drill, you have to put out more dummy piles than you have different colors of dummies, use different sizes or types as well as different colors. Perhaps you put out eighteen small plastic knobbies (six reds, six blacks, and six grays), and still have three more piles to stock. Use eighteen large plastic knobbies (red, black, and white). Or use three different kinds or sizes of canvas dummies.

Note on Administering Corrections

During these drills, especially at first, your dog will indeed suck to whatever distraction the specific drill includes. Actually, you want him to—so you can correct him. Until you've corrected him a few times, you can't be sure he is hearing the gospel you're preaching. So look on his mistakes as opportunities.

When he does suck to a distraction, let him get all the way to it, or almost there anyhow, before you correct him. Such corrections are called "hot-spotting" because they take advantage of the canine place-consciousness relative to punishment. Dogs are reluctant to return to places in which they have been chastised. So, when dealing with suction, you should delay the correction until your dog reaches the place you want him to avoid on the rerun. In lining drills, this means that you must either be extremely fleet of foot, or you must send him an e-mail message via the electronic collar.

In these suction drills, you shouldn't correct your dog so severely that he will never return to that place. Rather, you want to sting him just enough to keep him away during a couple of reruns. Then, you may want to send him to the place where you corrected him, especially if it is another dummy pile in a multi-legged pattern blind or the fall in a combination mark and blind drill. If you over-correct him in such an area, he won't return there even when you try to send him. (In fact, if he refuses to go to such a place on command, you should realize that you've over-corrected him. In such a case, you should relocate to a new area before proceeding.)

On the other hand, if you under-correct him, he will suck back again on the rerun. In such a case, you should "push the transmitter button harder" (increase the level of stimulation) in your correction, and then rerun the drill again. Eventually you'll get the correction about right. It's better to start with too little and build it up than to over-correct him immediately.

DRILLS

Multi-Legged Pattern Blind

Description

This trial-and-error drill has two or more pattern blinds extending as spokes from a common line (starting point). Each spoke should be at least 100 yards long. The diagram shows a three-legged layout with 45-degree angles. Eventually, many trainers advance their dogs to a five-legged layout. In either case, the trainer lines his dog successively to each dummy pile, but in no particular order. Before lining him to one pile, he *No*'s the dog off of the adjacent pile or piles. If the dog veers off and goes to the wrong dummy pile, the trainer corrects him just before he gets there, and then repeats the drill.

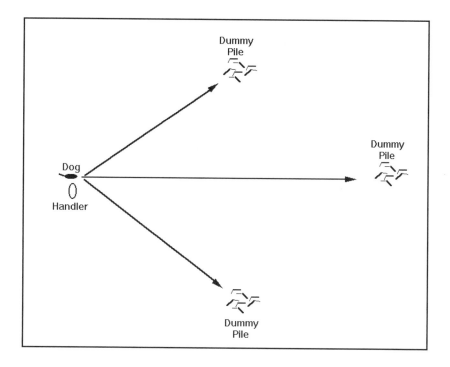

Figure 28. Multi-Legged Pattern Blind.

Purpose of Drill

This drill teaches your dog not to suck back to old blinds. In it, he learns to take whatever line you give him, even though he knows there are dummies in several locations.

It also teaches him what *No* means, relative to an incorrect picture. Through this drill, he learns that, when you *No* him off of one leg of the pattern field, he is not to go there, even though he knows he would find dummies. He learns that, in saying *No*, you aren't disputing the presence of those dummies. You're simply telling him they aren't the ones you want this time.

Prerequisites

Your dog should have learned to run single pattern blinds competently. He should have been e-collar-conditioned.

Equipment and Facilities

You need enough dummies for the number of dummy piles you intend to use. You need an e-collar, preferably with continuous stimulation.

Initially you need a flat, bare-ground or closely clipped field large enough for a three-legged pattern blind with each leg 100 yards long with 60-degree angles between adjacent legs. Later, you will need fields and lakes with appropriate hazards.

Precautions and Pitfalls

Don't send your dog to an empty dummy pile. (See *Note on Stocking the Dummy Piles*, above.)

Don't over-correct your dog with the e-collar. (See *Note on Administering Corrections*, above.)

Don't overwork your dog in any one session. Remember that every time you say *Back*, he runs 200 yards.

Process—Steps in Training

Start out in a bare-ground or closely clipped area. Set up the pattern blinds, initially with only two legs at 60 degrees, laid out so your dog will be running generally downwind as he goes toward the dummy piles. Identify the dummy piles for your dog (see *Note on Identifying the Dummy Piles*, above).

Now, set him up facing either pile—and *No* him off of it. (See

Handling Techniques, above.) Re-heel him to face the other pile, let him lock in on it, go through your blind retrieve sequence, and send him. If he veers off and heads for the wrong dummy pile, correct him as described in *Note on Administering Corrections*, above. (If he actually picks up a dummy from the wrong pile, don't worry about it; let him bring it on it to you.)

Go back and forth between the two legs of your pattern blind. Each time, *No* him off of one pile and send him to the other. After he has mastered this two-legged pattern blind, add a third leg. Initially keep the angles at least 60 degrees. Later you may or may not want to reduce the angles to 45 degrees, and perhaps add two more legs.

You can set this drill up quickly almost anywhere. So, as your dog progresses, you should incorporate all sorts of terrain and cover hazards. You should set it up partially in water, and eventually totally in water. Of course, since these are pattern blinds, whenever you move to a new location, you must identify each pile for your dog before drilling him.

Addenda

This is the cornerstone drill for suction-proofing. After your dog has learned that he shouldn't suck back to the wrong dummy pile ("old blinds") in this drill, he will learn much more quickly and easily not to suck back to old falls and other distractions.

Wagon Wheel

Description

The layout for this trial-and-error drill looks like a wagon wheel. With the dog sitting at heel, the trainer stands at the hub and tosses dummies evenly around the rim of an imaginary wheel surrounding them. Then he lines the dog to this and that dummy. After he delivers each dummy, the trainer tosses it back where it was, so the rim is always fully stocked.

To be effective, this drill requires at least eight dummies in the wheel, which puts a 45-degree angle between each adjacent pair. Most trainers prefer to work their dogs up to a 16-dummy wagon wheel, which has angles of only 22.5 degrees. Some trainers, primarily field trialers, who need very precise lining, extend this drill to a 32-dummy wagon wheel, with angles of 11.25 degrees! For hunting and hunting test folks,

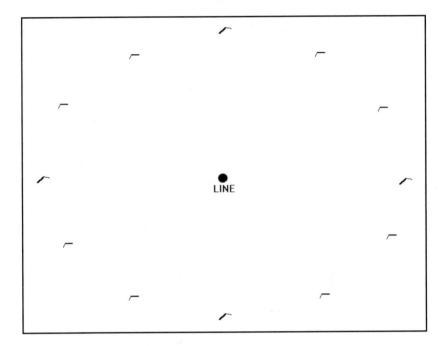

Figure 29. Twelve-Spoked Wagon Wheel.

eight dummies are the minimum, and 12 to 16 are ideal. (There is no rule that says a person *must* start with 4, then double that to 8, then again double it to 16. You can toss out whatever number of dummies you choose.)

Most trainers, when they advance beyond eight dummies, turn this drill into a double-rimmed affair, in which the dummies lie on two rims, one at about ten yards and the other at about fifteen yards, with each dummy on the other rim from those on either side of it. This forces the dog to ignore two nearer dummies every time he is sent for a dummy on the outside rim.

Purpose of Drill

This drill teaches your dog to take fine lines to the dummy you select. Since the retrieves are very short (10 to 15 yards), he can do a lot of them in one session, thereby accelerating the learning process.

Prerequisites

Your dog should be competent in the three-legged multi-legged pattern blind drill, above. He should have been e-collar-conditioned.

Equipment and Facilities

You need 12 to 16 small white and 6 to 8 small red dummies. You need an e-collar, preferably with momentary stimulation.

You need a bare-ground or closely clipped area that is at least 40 yards by 40 yards.

Precautions and Pitfalls

Don't over-correct your dog with the e-collar.   (See *Note on Administering Corrections,* above.)

Don't push your dog too rapidly from the 4-dummy to the 8-dummy drill, or from the 8-dummy drill to the 12- or 16-dummy drill. Make sure he understands each level before increasing the number of dummies. Similarly, don't advance him to the double-rimmed drill until he can handle the single-rimmed drill with the same number of dummies.

Don't overwork your dog in any one session.

Process—Steps in Training

Start out with four white dummies. Toss them out at 90-degree angles around the rim of the circle. Now, choose one—*not* the last one thrown, which would be too easy—and line your dog to it, with your normal blind retrieve sequence. If he veers off for one of the other dummies, which is unlikely with them so widely separated, nick him with the e-collar just before he reaches it, and call him back in. (If he brings the wrong dummy back, don't fret about it; simply toss it back where it belongs.) *No* him off the dummy he just went after (see *Handling Techniques*, above) and set him up for the one he should have gone for. Now heel him a couple of steps toward the correct dummy and send him for it again. He'll get it this time. When he delivers it, toss it back where it was, *No* him off of it, set him up facing a different dummy, and send him for it with your normal blind retrieve sequence. And so on for all four dummies. Do this until he regularly goes for the dummy you select, without correction. If possible, change locations from one session to the next.

Next toss out six or eight white dummies, all about the same distance from the hub. Line him to each one of them, correcting his mistakes as explained above. When he takes your line in this drill consistently (which will take a few sessions), mix three or four of the less visible red dummies in with four white ones. Make every other dummy red, but keep them all about the same distance from the hub. When you send him for a red one, he will be strongly tempted to go to one of the more visible white ones on either side. (As an intermediate step, you might mix in black dummies instead of red ones. The blacks are more visible than reds, so your dog will "get it" faster with blacks. Then replace the blacks with reds.) Whenever he errs, correct him as described above.

After he learns to do this single-circle drill with six or eight dummies consistently well, toss the red dummies about half again as far as its two white "neighbors." That will give you an inner circle of three or four white dummies at about 10 yards and an outer circle of three or four red dummies at about 15 yards.

When your dog performs correctly on this double-rimmed wagon wheel with six or eight dummies, you can double the number to 12 or 16. Start with all white dummies, all at about the same distance. Watch your dog's head and eyes closely to make sure he has locked in on the proper dummy before you send him. If he locks in on the wrong dummy, *No* him off of it and set him up again (see *Handling Techniques*, above). When he can handle the single-rimmed drill with 12 or 16 dummies with all white dummies, intersperse red and white dummies, still all at the same distance. And, of course, finally, toss the red ones about half again as far as the whites.

Addenda

This is an excellent "quickie drill" to teach the dog that you are serious about the line you give him. It takes little space and not too much time per session.

Pattern Blind with a White Object Distraction

Description

All dogs, whether or not they were trained to line and cast with visual aids, will suck to white objects until trained not to. This drill facilitates curing this tendency in dogs that have been trained to line and cast with white visual aids. The next drill, Pattern Blind with Distraction, should be used for dogs trained to line and cast without visual aids.

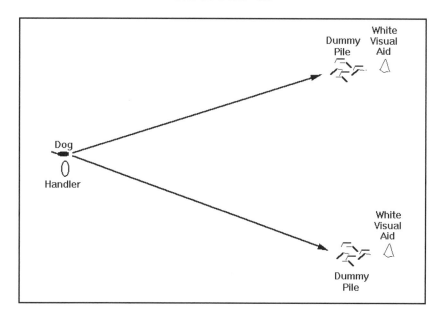

Figure 30. Pattern Blind with White Distraction.

In this current drill, the trainer first runs his dog on a double visual aid pattern blind. Then, he picks up one of the visual aids and leaves the other in place. He *No*'s his dog off the remaining visual aid and lines him to the dummy pile without a visual aid. If the dog sucks back to the visual aid in sight, the trainer corrects him just before he reaches it. Then he reruns the drill, starting again by *No*-ing his dog off of the visual aid. If he takes the correct line this time, which he probably will, the trainer next lines him to the visual dummy pile—and then to the other dummy pile, the one without a visual aid. He goes back and forth like this several times, to convince the dog that he is to run to a visual aid only when sent to it.

After drilling the dog adequately with visual aids this way, the trainer introduces other white objects: plastic bleach bottles, large snow goose or pintail decoys, a chair draped with a white cloth, and so on. However, he doesn't use these other white objects to mark a dummy pile. He simply puts them out as distractions to be ignored.

Purpose of Drill

This drill teaches the dog trained to line and cast with visual aids to ignore white objects when the boss so indicates.

Prerequisites

Your dog should be competent in the multi-legged pattern blind drill with visual aids. He should have been e-collar-conditioned.

Equipment and Facilities

You need enough dummies for two dummy piles, and you need two visual aids. Eventually, you will want to use various other white objects (whatever your imagination suggests). You need an e-collar, preferably with continuous stimulation.

Initially, you need a flat, bare-ground or closely clipped field at least 100 yards by 50 yards. Later, you will also be able to use areas with various cover and terrain variations. Finally, you can run this drill in water.

Precautions and Pitfalls

Don't send your dog to an empty dummy pile. (See *Note on Stocking the Dummy Piles*, above.)

Don't over-correct your dog with the e-collar. (See *Note on Administering Corrections*, above.)

Don't overwork your dog in any one session.

Process—Steps in Training

On a flat, bare-ground or closely clipped field, set up a wide-angled downwind double pattern blind with visual aids. Line your dog to each pile twice. Remove one visual aid, but leave everything else (both dummy piles and the other visual aid) in place. *No* your dog off the remaining visual aid, and set him up to take a line to the other dummy pile, the one from which the visual aid has been removed. (See *Handling Techniques*, above.) Send him. If he sucks over to the remaining visual aid, let him get all the way there before correcting him. (See *Note on Administering Corrections*, above.) Whistle him back in to you. (If he brings a dummy, don't fret; just toss it behind you.) Now, repeat the process, starting with *No*-ing him off of the visual aid. This time he will probably take your line, but if he sucks back again, zap him again, perhaps a bit harder, and repeat the drill.

After he successfully takes your line to the dummy pile without a visual aid, send him back to the other dummy pile, the one marked by the visual aid. If he refuses to go there, he's telling you that you over-corrected him, in which case you should relocate and lighten up on the juice before proceeding. But, if he takes your line to the dummy pile with the visual aid, great! Next, you should again *No* him off of the visual aid and send him to the other dummy pile again. And so on.

Change locations often. After he does this drill reliably (without correction) on bare ground, move into cover. Set the drill up in places with various cover and terrain variations. When he handles it well in all the cover and terrain situations you feel necessary, introduce various white objects as the distraction instead of the visual aid. Set up a single pattern blind with a visual aid and put any white object as a distraction off to the side. Line your dog to the visual aid once or twice. Then remove the visual aid. *No* your dog off of the distraction and send him for the dummy pile. And so on.

Next set this drill up in water, first with a double pattern blind with visual aids, then as a single pattern blind with white object distractions. After all the preparatory work, he should have no problem in water. He should require no corrections, which is why you saved water for last. The less frequently you have to correct him in water, the more he will enjoy water work.

Addenda

The last phases of this drill, when you work your dog with various white object distractions, is really a form of the following drill.

Pattern Blind with a Distraction

Description

This trial-and-error drill trains the dog to ignore various distractions that would normally incline him to veer off of the line the boss has given him. In it, the trainer introduces a variety of visual and audible distractions into his dog's pattern blinds. He first *No*'s his dog off of the distraction, then lines him to the pattern blind. If the dog sucks to the distraction, the trainer corrects him just before he reaches it. Then he reruns the entire drill, to make sure the dog "caught his drift." By introducing a variety of distractions this way, the trainer can gradually condition his dog to "take *No* for an answer."

Purpose of Drill

This drill conditions your dog to take the line you give him and to

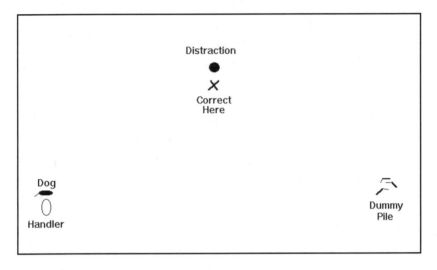

Figure 31. Pattern Blind with a Distraction.

ignore attractive visual and aural distractions.

Nota bene: If you have trained your dog with visual aid pattern blinds, you can more effectively cure him of sucking to white objects with the above drill, Pattern Blind with White Object Distraction.

Prerequisites

Your dog should be competent in the multi-legged pattern blind, above. He should have been e-collar-conditioned.

Equipment and Facilities

You need enough dummies for one dummy pile. To mark the dummy pile, you need either a visual aid or an assistant. You need a variety of distractions, whatever you think you might encounter in hunting or dog-games. You need an e-collar, preferably with continuous stimulation.

Initially you need a bare-ground or closely clipped area of appropriate size for your pattern blind and distraction setup. Later, you'll want to run this drill in various locations with terrain and cover hazards. You don't really need water, for if you cure your dog on land, the training will carry over to water, too. However, you may want to test him in water occasionally, just to make sure.

Precautions and Pitfalls

Don't send your dog to an empty dummy pile. (See *Note on Stocking the Dummy Piles*, above.)

Don't over-correct your dog with the e-collar. (See *Note on Administering Corrections*, above.)

Don't overwork your dog in any one session.

Process—Steps in Training

Set up a downwind pattern blind in a flat, bare-ground or closely clipped field. Identify the dummy pile for your dog. (See *Note on Identifying the Dummy Piles*, above.) Now, add a distraction. Perhaps a good first one would be an assistant standing about halfway to the dummy pile and about 20 yards off-line to either side. Heel your dog to the line and *No* him off the distraction (see *Handling Techniques*, above). Set him up for the pattern blind, and send him. If he sucks over to the distraction, correct him as described in *Note on Administering Corrections*, above. Then, either handle him to the pattern blind or call him back to you. If you do the latter, heel him about a third of the way toward the dummy pile. There, again *No* him off of the distraction, then set him up for the pattern blind and send him. When he delivers, return to the original line (starting point) and rerun the entire test.

Change locations and distractions often. Incorporate other terrain and cover hazards.

Addenda

As mentioned above, curing your dog of sucking to distractions on land will also cure him in water. Nevertheless, you should check him out in water, too, before you finish with this drill.

Pattern Blind with a Mark at an Angle

Description

This trial-and-error drill trains a retriever to ignore old falls when running a blind retrieve. In both hunting and dog-games, the location of a previous mark is the most challenging "distraction" during a blind retrieve. Until trained otherwise, a dog will suck to such an old fall like a moth to a flame.

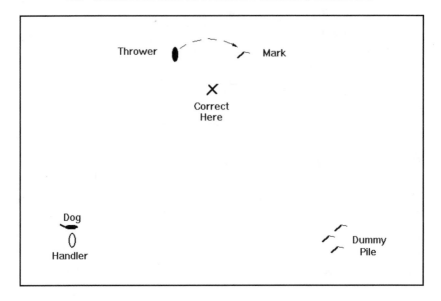

Figure 32. Pattern Blind with a Mark at an Angle.

This drill consists of a single pattern blind with a single marked retrieve, at an angle from the line to the blind. The trainer normally sends his dog for the mark first, then lines him to the blind (after *No*-ing him off of the area of the mark). Initially, he sets this drill up on bare ground with a wide angle between the mark and the blind. As his dog progresses, he narrows the angle until it is quite snug. Then he moves into cover and starts over with a wide angle—narrowing it down as his dog's progress indicates.

Occasionally, instead of sending him to pick up the mark first, the trainer reverses the test. He doesn't let the dog pick up the mark until after he has completed the pattern blind. This makes the mark a much stronger temptation.

Purpose of Drill

This is the bread-and-butter pattern blind drill for curing a dog of sucking to marks, whether "old falls" that have been retrieved, or "fresh falls" that are still on the ground.

Prerequisites

Your dog should be competent at multi-legged pattern blinds, and should have been "suction-proofed" relative to various sights and sounds through the above drill, Pattern Blind with a Distraction. He should have been e-collar-conditioned.

Equipment and Facilities

You need enough dummies for one dummy pile and one mark. To identify the dummy pile for your dog, you need either a visual aid or an assistant. To throw the mark, you need either an assistant or a dummy launcher. You need an e-collar, preferably with continuous stimulation.

Initially, you need a flat, bare-ground or closely clipped field at least 100 yards by 50 yards. Later, you will need training areas with various terrain and cover hazards. Eventually you will need suitable water.

Precautions and Pitfalls

Don't send your dog to an empty dummy pile. (See *Note on Stocking the Dummy Piles*, above.)

Don't over-correct your dog with the e-collar. (See *Note on Administering Corrections*, above.)

Don't narrow the angle between the mark and the blind too quickly, especially after you move into cover.

Don't overwork your dog in any one session.

Process—Steps in Training

In a flat, bare-ground or closely clipped field, set up a downwind single pattern blind with a single marked retrieve at an angle of at least 60 degrees. Identify the dummy pile for your dog (see *Identifying the Dummy Piles*, above). Now have the mark thrown and send your dog to retrieve it. After he delivers the dummy, *No* him off of the mark (see *Handling Techniques*, above), and set him up to run the pattern blind. Send him. If he sucks back to the mark (now an "old fall"), let him get all the way there before correcting him (see *Administering Corrections*, above). Call him back in to you. Again *No* him off of the mark, and send him for the pattern blind. (If he again sucks back to the mark, which is unlikely, correct him again, but with a little more juice.) After he takes the correct line to the pattern blind, rerun the entire test (mark and pattern blind) once or twice. (If he refuses to go to the area of the mark, you have over-corrected him there. Change locations and back off a bit on the juice.) After he has mastered the concept, you should occasionally— about once in ten times—have the mark thrown, but run the pattern blind first. This is a stronger temptation, so be prepared to correct him on these even if he is doing well in the tests with the more normal mark-then-blind sequence.

Gradually narrow the angle until the mark is falling only about 15 yards from the line to the pattern blind. When he takes a good line to the pattern blind even then, he's ready to move into cover. In running this test in cover, make the mark quite simple. The simpler it is the more he will be tempted to suck back to it. (Also, the more difficult it is, the longer he will spend hunting for it, and the more energy he will expend.) Of course, start out with the mark at a wide angle from the pattern blind. As his responses indicate, narrow the angle between the mark and the blind, but don't make them as snug as you did on bare ground. And always put the mark in a location where its scent will not blow toward the dog as he takes the line to the pattern blind.

When he is doing good work in various cover situations, run this drill in water.

Addenda

This drill has some fairly obvious applications and extensions, especially for dog-games, which should be mentioned:

1. When you run this drill in reverse order by picking up the blind before the mark, you are preparing your dog for one type of the two types of "poison bird" tests. This is a good idea, because such situations do come up in hunting and are often used in dog-games. The other type of "poison bird" test makes a lot less sense, but since some dog-game judges use it, I'll describe it. In it, the blind is planted rather close to the edge of the area of the fall for the mark. The dog must pick up the mark before being sent for the blind, so the bird for the blind is there on the ground while the dog hunts for the mark. If he strays from the area of the fall while hunting for the mark, he may well stumble on the blind and thereby eliminate himself. Thus, if a dog leaves the area of the fall, the handler must immediately handle him to the bird. Handling on a mark is penalized in dog-games, but not as severely as stumbling on a blind while hunting for a mark. So, this is a trick test intended to trap dogs into making a mistake of greater or lesser severity. I don't like this second type of "poison bird" test, but it happens. Unfortunately, no drill exists to allow you to train for it. Oh, well.

2. If, in this drill, you were to have the mark fall directly on the path to the blind, you would be preparing your dog (as much as possible) for another trick test. Although I don't like it, in dog-games, it's some considerable distance from unheard of. Thus, you should run this test that way occasionally in training. All it really proves is whether you can handle your dog out of all the scent that accumulates on the line to the blind after several marks (real birds) have been thrown there. In preparing your dog for such a test, do it first with dummies, and then with birds.

3. You can extend this drill to a double blind with a single mark either between the two blinds or off to either side. You can extend it to a double or triple mark with the blind located between the falls or on either side. And, of course, you can extend it to a double or triple mark with a two or three blinds laced through and around the marks. All of these are important dog-game tests, which also occur at least occasionally in hunting.

4. The following drill, Pattern Blind under the Arc of a Fall, is just an extension of this drill, albeit an advanced one.

Pattern Blind under the Arc of a Fall

Description

In this trial-and-error drill, the pattern blind is set up so the line to it runs directly under the arc of the fall for the accompanying mark. This is a severe suction test, for the dog must run between the gunners and the area of the fall. Although such a sequence of retrieves can happen in hunting, it isn't common. However, this type of test comes up often enough in dog-games to justify training for it with this drill.

The trainer sets up a combination pattern blind and mark test. He positions the thrower for the mark so he stands on one side of the line to the pattern blind dummy pile where he can throw the mark so it falls on the opposite side of that line. Normally, the trainer sends his dog for the mark first, and then the blind. Eventually, of course, to make the test even more difficult, he occasionally reverses the order, sending him first for the blind, then for the mark. Either way, the mark is thrown before the dog is sent the first time.

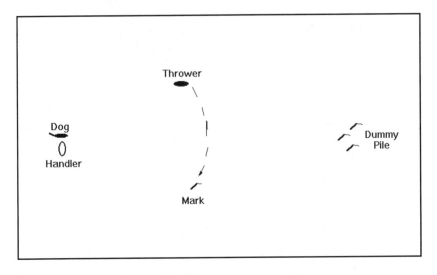

Figure 33. Pattern Blind under Arc of a Fall.

Purpose of Drill

This drill prepares your dog for dog-game tests in which the line to a blind runs under the arc of a mark.

Prerequisites

Your dog should be proficient at the following two suction drills: Pattern Blind with Distraction (especially with a person as the distraction) and Pattern Blind with a Mark at an Angle. He should have been e-collar-conditioned.

Equipment and Facilities

You need enough dummies for one dummy pile and a single mark. To identify the dummy pile for your dog, you need either a visual aid or an assistant. To throw the mark, you need an assistant, with or without a dummy launcher. (A dummy launcher by itself wouldn't offer the same level of distraction that the person would.) Eventually, you should run this test with a bird for the mark, preferably a flier. For such a flier, you need at least one assistant who is a good (and safe) shot. You need an e-collar, preferably with continuous stimulation.

Initially, you need a flat, bare-ground or closely clipped field at least 100 yards by 50 yards. Later on, you should also run this test in various cover situations, and even in water.

Precautions and Pitfalls

Don't send your dog to an empty dummy pile. (See *Note on Stocking the Dummy Piles*, above.)

Don't over-correct your dog with the e-collar. (See *Note on Administering Corrections*, above.)

Don't overwork your dog in any one session.

Process—Steps in Training

In a flat, bare-ground or closely clipped field, set up a downwind single pattern blind and identify the dummy pile for your dog. (See *Note on Identifying the Dummy Piles*, above.) Now position your assistant near enough to the line to the pattern blind so he can throw easily to the other side. Put him out about halfway to the pattern blind. Have him throw the mark and send your dog to retrieve it. When he returns, *No* him off the area of the mark (see *Handling Techniques*, above) and send him for the pattern blind. If he sucks to the old fall (or thrower), let him get all the way there before you correct him (see *Note on Administering Corrections*, above). Then call him back in to you. Again *No* him off of the old fall (or thrower) and send him for the pattern blind. (If he sucks back again, which is unlikely, repeat the correction, but up the juice a tad.) After he successfully lines the pattern blind, rerun the entire test. (If he refuses to go to the area of the mark to retrieve it, you have over-corrected him. Change locations and lighten up on the juice.)

Change locations frequently. After he runs this test without correction consistently, occasionally—about once every ten times—reverse the order of the retrieves. Have the mark thrown, then send your dog for the pattern blind. After he delivers it, send him for the mark.

Next, have your assistant throw a dead bird instead of a dummy. For this, you need a strong-armed assistant or, better yet, a dummy launcher. (If you use the latter, have an assistant standing near it, to increase the attractiveness of the gunner station for your dog.) After your dog masters this test with a dead bird, start using live fliers (provided your assistant is a decent shot).

With all that accomplished on bare ground, start running this drill in cover, starting with dummies, and advancing to dead, then live birds. In cover, make the marks easy, so your dog won't waste too much time and energy finding them.

Finally, run this test in water.

Addenda

In a sense, this drill is an extension of the above Pattern Blind with Mark at an Angle drill. However, this is a much more difficult test.

With the right kind of launcher (one that throws a bird a long, long way), you can extend this test to a double blind under the arc of a single fall. Tough, tough test.

11
Transition Drills

Chapters 4 through 8 describe drills for conditioning your dog to perform each of the three parts of a blind retrieve (lining, stopping, and casting). Chapter 9 describes drills that combine two or all three of those parts. Chapter 10 describes drills to cure your dog of sucking to old blinds, old falls, and miscellaneous other distractions. However, in none of these drills does your dog have the slightest doubt about where the dummy piles are.

Between those drills, in which your dog knows where he's going, and real blind retrieves, in which he doesn't, lurks a sizeable chasm. Clearly, you need a bridge over that chasm, a bridge that will convince your dog that he doesn't need to know where he's going, that you'll direct him to the bird if he'll just do what you have already trained him to do.

This chapter gives you that bridge. In fact, it gives you two such bridges, one for land, the other for water. In each, you instill the necessary "blind faith" your dog must have in you. You do this gradually, in small increments, and always in trial-and-success mode. Not surprisingly, you should cross the land bridge first, and then the water bridge. The land bridge consists of two drills: the dummy string blind and the pop-up blind. The first enables you to begin running real blind retrieves on land. The second allows you to extend real blinds to considerable distances without damaging your dog's confidence. The water bridge, the thrown blind, does "all of the above" for water blinds. Through these bridging drills, you'll see all your previous blind retrieve drilling (and drilling, and drilling, and drilling) come together into a unified mosaic of canine art. Thereafter, your dog will begin to do blind retrieves that may amaze even you.

DRILLS

Dummy String Blind

Description

This trial-and-success drill introduces a retriever to real blind retrieves on land, in a gradual and totally positive way. In a flat field with light cover, the trainer sets his dog up for a blind retrieve and sends him off, he (the dog) knows not where. From rote conditioning, he takes off and begins to run. When he has gone no more than 20 yards, lo and behold, he stumbles on a dummy! In fact, if he's at all observant, he'll notice he has chanced upon a mother lode of dummies, all laid out in a long string perpendicular to the line he took.

When he delivers the dummy, he doesn't notice that the trainer is about 20 yards farther away from the dummy string than he was before. So, now the trainer sets his dog up and sends him again, this time from 40 yards. Since the dog knows where the dummies are, he runs straight to them again. When he delivers, he finds the trainer 60 yards from the dummy string. And so on.

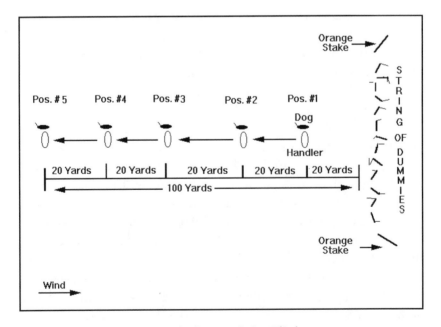

Figure 34. Dummy String Blind.

In each subsequent session, always in different locations, the trainer makes the initial run longer—40 yards—60 yards—80 yards—100 yards—and so on. Also, in each subsequent session, he makes the dummy string shorter and shorter—until the dummy string becomes a dummy pile. At some point in this process, the dog will miss the dummy string (or pile) completely and keep on running. Wonderful! Just what the trainer wants! He blows the *Stop*-whistle, and handles the dog to the dummy pile, as a real blind retrieve.

Thereafter, the dummy string is no longer necessary. The trainer simply puts out a dummy pile and establishes a line. He gradually adds complexity—terrain, cover, and wind hazards, suction factors, and so forth—to these real blind retrieves (for such they have become through this gradual process).

Purpose of Drill

This drill helps your dog make the transition from drills in which he knows the location of the dummy piles to real blind retrieves on land.

Prerequisites

First, your dog should have been so thoroughly drilled in lining that, when sent, he will absolutely, positively run at least 25 or 30 yards before wondering why he's doing it. Second, he should have been so thoroughly drilled in stopping that he *always* sits on the whistle—and as the late George Mitchell used to say, "Always is a lot of times!" Finally, he should have been so thoroughly drilled in casting that he will absolutely, positively take your casts.

Equipment and Facilities

You need at least 30 dark dummies to lay out a dummy string 15 yards long, with no more than 18 inches between dummies. You need two small orange stakes with which to mark the ends of the dummy string (for you, not for your dog). They should be tall enough so you can see them from a distance, but not so tall that they become silhouetted against the sky for your dog.

You need a flat field at least 100 yards by 30 yards with fairly even light cover. Actually, you need several such locations, so you can change "venues" each session.

Precautions and Pitfalls

Always run this drill straight downwind. If you were to run it upwind, your dog would scent the dummies too soon. Also, lining an inexperienced dog into the wind encourages quartering, which you don't want in blind retrieves.

Don't use white dummies. They are so highly visible that your dog might see them from the line before his initial run, especially at first when his initial runs are so short. Small black dummies are ideal, for your dog can't see them from any distance at all, but when he nears the dummy string, he will be able to see black dummies more easily than red ones (or those of any other neutral color).

The distances given here for the initial run in each session are not absolutes. If your dog doesn't react properly—if he acts confused—shorten up, and proceed more slowly with shorter incremental increases in distances. Keep this drill positive and enjoyable for him. A short success is better than a long failure.

If, on his initial run, your dog runs somewhat crooked, but still is headed toward some part of the dummy string, don't fret. Let him go. You put out a long string to compensate for the fact that beginning dogs often do indeed take crooked lines.

On each rerun, your dog will return to the same spot in the string where he found a dummy the first time. So, if he ran crooked the first time, he will do it again on all subsequent reruns in the same session. Again, don't fret about it. In fact, you should capitalize on this trait, turn it into a training trick. How? By lining him in reruns to the spot in the string he hit on his initial run. That way, in his mind, he will be taking the line you are giving him. This is subtle conditioning, and it works.

Keep the dummy string well stocked. By going to the same spot two or three times, your dog will create a "hole" he might later run straight through. You don't want that, so after every two or three retrieves, put him up for a rest while you replenish your dummy string.

Don't overwork your dog in any one session.

Process—Steps in Training

In a flat field with light cover, lay out a dummy string 15 yards long, with no more than 18 inches between dummies. Lay it out across the prevailing wind. Don't let your dog watch you do this. He shouldn't know where the dummies are before his initial run.

Heel your dog to a point about 20 yards straight upwind from the center of the string, and have him sit facing it. Go through your blind retrieve sequence and send him. Having done a seemingly a zillion pattern blinds of 100 yards or more, his conditioned response to your *Back* will carry him at least 25 or 30 yards before his conscious mind kicks in. By then he will either see or smell one of the dummies. He may not take your line precisely. He may angle a bit this way or that, but with any reasonable initial line, he will run smack into the dummy string.

(When your dog picks up a dummy, you and he will have done your first real blind retrieve. Granted, it was only 20 yards long, but it was truly a blind retrieve, not a pattern blind. Congratulations! Only a small percentage of those who set out to train a retriever actually reach this point.)

As your dog goes toward the dummy string in this initial run, you should run back the other way about 20 yards. That way, when he delivers the first dummy, you can rerun him from 40 yards, and he'll hardly notice the difference. Since he now knows where the dummies are, all reruns in this session become pattern blinds. However, they prepare him for the longer initial run in the subsequent session. As he runs toward the dummy string from 40 yards, you should run back another 20 yards, so the next rerun will be from 60 yards. Following the same procedure, his fourth run will be from 80 yards, and his fifth and final one from 100 yards.

Your next session should be in a new location, so his first run will again be a real blind retrieve. Lay out the same dummy string, but this time run him initially from 40 yards instead of 20. As he goes toward the dummy string, you should run back another 30 yards, so you can rerun him from 70 yards. As he goes to the string this time, you should run back another 30 yards and rerun him from 100 yards. You should limit his retrieves in this drill to five per session. So, after this third run, you should either continue to lengthen him out or rerun him from 100 yards, whichever better suits your personal goals.

In your next session, in a new location, shorten the dummy string to 10 yards long, and run your dog initially from 50 yards. Then, rerun him from 75 and 100 yards, and so on.

In each subsequent session (always in new locations), lengthen your dog's initial run by 5 or 10 yards, until it is 100 yards (or whatever maximum you desire). Also, in each session, shorten the dummy string by 2 or 3 yards, until it becomes just a pile. At some time in this process, your dog will miss the dummies completely and sail on past them. When he does, toot your whistle and wave your arms. (Translation: "Handle" him to the pile. Stop him with the *Stop*-whistle and give him an *Over*. When he's directly beyond the dummies, stop him again, then give him a *Come-in*. Bingo!)

(For the first time, you and your dog have combined lining, stopping, and casting in a real blind retrieve! Congratulations! Hang it up for the day. Go home, feed your dog something special, and take your spouse out for dinner. In just the right restaurant, said spouse will listen patiently while your monologue runs the gamut from extreme modesty through self-congratulations and finally all the way to profound wisdom. Enjoy! You've earned it!)

Thereafter, you can dispense with the dummy string. Simply put out a dummy pile. And you can gradually add complexity to your dog's real blind retrieves, for that he is now running. You and he have crossed the bridge, made the transition!

Addenda

However, having made the transition, you shouldn't abandon the basic lining, stopping, and casting drills that brought you to this point. All through your dog's active life, you should continue to use them for several purposes: to teach him new concepts; to correct problems that develop in his real blind retrieves (popping, scalloping, refusals of various kinds, and so on); and to build or rebuild his confidence from time to time.

Pop-Up Blind

Description

In this trial-and-success drill, the trainer sends his dog on a line to a blind that is a bit too long for him. Then, just before the dog's confidence begins to flag, a dummy pops up some distance in front of him and falls on a patch of relatively bare ground. He races in, picks it up and brings it back.

Purpose of Drill

You can use this drill for three related purposes: first, to extend the distance you can line your dog without risk of failure; second, to

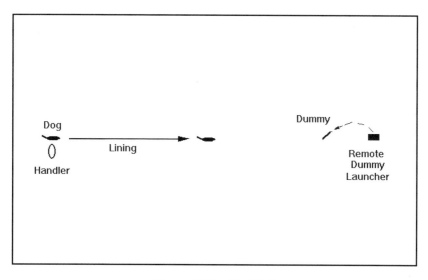

Figure 35. Pop-Up Blind.

re-establish his confidence whenever he seems to need it; and third, to help overcome a popping problem.

Prerequisites

Your dog should be running real blind retrieves on land reasonably well.

Equipment and Facilities

You need a small white dummy. You need a remote-control bird launcher to make the dummy pop up at just the right time. If absolutely necessary, you could also use a hidden dummy launcher or a hidden assistant to throw the dummy. However, these latter two methods normally require long throws from substantial hiding places on one side or the other of the line to the blind. Such throws encourage your dog, as he runs, to swing his head from side to side looking for the dummy. That, in turn, encourages him to run zig-zag lines instead of straight ones. However, you can set up the easily hidden little bird launcher very near the intended spot for the blind. From there, it can pop the dummy straight up and down, thereby encouraging your dog to look straight ahead as he runs.

Initially you need fairly flat field, at least 100 yards long, with light cover. It should have a patch of bare ground where the dummy lands, so your dog doesn't have to hunt for it when he gets there. Later, you can run this drill in various terrain and cover situations, but always with a bare-ground patch for the dummy to land in.

Precautions and Pitfalls

Tilt the bird launcher slightly toward the line, so it will throw the dummy toward the dog as he approaches the launcher. Your dog shouldn't get involved with the launcher itself in this drill, lest he injure himself somehow. If it throws the dummy toward him so it lands on bare ground, your dog will pick the dummy up before reaching the launcher.

Make sure the dummy lands in a bare-ground patch, where your dog won't have to hunt for it. (Hunting, instead of carrying lines and casts, on a blind retrieve can become a nasty habit.) Test fire the launcher before bringing your dog to the line, to make sure the dummy takes the right trajectory and lands in the bare-ground area.

Don't wait too long to pop the dummy up. Do it while your dog is still running his line. If you wait until he begins to give up, he may look away and not see the dummy.

Don't overwork your dog in any one session.

Process—Steps in Training

Set the drill up according to the diagram. Heel your dog to the line and set him up. Go through your blind retrieve sequence and send him. Let him carry the line a reasonable distance before you push the button that fires the bird launcher. However, don't wait until he has slowed down, veered off, or otherwise given signs of losing confidence. When he sees the dummy, he will accelerate toward it, pick up it up, and return to you.

If, on his initial run, you had to launch the dummy before he lined very far, you should rerun him immediately. To do so, put him up while you reload the bird launcher, then heel him to the line again and start over. This time, since he knows where the dummy will be, he should run much farther before you launch the dummy. But don't let him get so close before you fire it that the noise of the launcher might startle him.

Thereafter, run this drill in different locations and with different hazards. Wherever you set it up, be sure your dog can see the dummy pop up anywhere along his line to it. Also be sure you can see him at all times, so you'll know when to launch the dummy.

Addenda

This drill is similar to the following Thrown Blind drill for water blinds. However, it doesn't involve a long throw, so doesn't damage your dog's straight lines the way a thrown blind would on land.

In an ideal situation, you could set this drill up in water. However, you shouldn't do so until after you have introduced your dog to real water blinds with the following thrown blind drill.

Thrown Blind

Description

This trial-and-success drill introduces a retriever to real water blinds as gently and surely as the above dummy string blind drill introduces him to real land blinds. In it, the trainer uses precisely timed thrown dummies, tossed by either a hidden assistant or a hidden dummy launcher, to lead his dog gradually into longer and longer swims before the dummy appears.

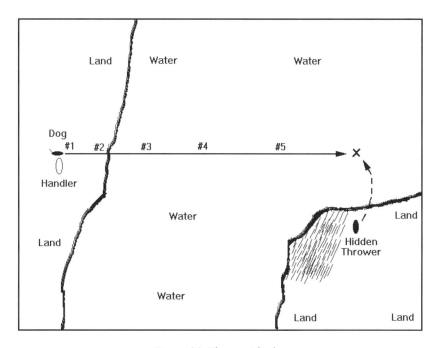

Figure 36. Thrown Blind.

Purpose of Drill

This drill introduces the dog to real water blinds, without correction and with almost no risk of failure.

Prerequisites

The dog should have been drilled extensively in pattern blinds, stopping drills, and casting drills, in water as well as on land. He should be reasonably competent in real blinds on land. If he has had pop-up blinds on land, he will grasp the concept of this drill very quickly.

Equipment and Facilities

You need several large white dummies. You have three options for having the dummy thrown. First, you can use a hidden assistant, who will throw the dummy when you signal him. Second, you can use a hidden single-shot dummy launcher with a hidden assistant nearby to keep it loaded. Third, you can use a hidden multi-shot dummy launcher without an attending assistant.

If you use an assistant, a pair of 2-way radios would be nice for communications, although not absolutely necessary.

You need a suitable pond. Actually, you need several ponds or several places on larger lakes. To be suitable, each location must have a properly located hiding place for your assistant and/or dummy launcher. In this drill, the swims should be relatively short, perhaps no more than 50 yards, so you can do several reruns per session.

Precautions and Pitfalls

Don't let your dog see your assistant or your dummy launcher at any time. Not when you heel him to the line. Not when he sits at the line. Not when he swims to the dummy. Not when he swims back with the dummy. If your dog sees your assistant, it will magnify his natural suction proclivities, especially to old falls and people standing here or there. For the same reason, don't let your dog hear your assistant at any time. If your assistant must talk to you, he should do so through a pair of 2-way radios. Lacking those, have him signal you somehow to put your dog up while he speaks.

If you have an assistant throwing the dummies, you need a very clear and distinct signal for indicating when you want him to throw one. In this drill, nothing is more frustrating than not getting a throw when your dog really needs one. And the second most frustrating thing is being surprised by an unexpected (and therefore unwanted) throw. When running this drill with an assistant throwing, I've always waved my hat high above my head as a signal for him to throw.

Never delay too long before initiating a throw. Don't wait until your dog gives up and heads back toward you, for he won't see the throw then. Signal for it when he is still driving in the proper direction. When your dog understands the drill and swims confidently all the way, don't delay the throw until he reaches the spot where the dummy will fall, lest it hit him or splashes so close that it frightens him.

Have the dummy thrown so it lands in the water in front of your dog. If you have it thrown so it lands on land, it will encourage water cheating.

Don't continue this drill any longer than necessary. In most suitable locations, the throw will come from one side or the other, rather than from dead ahead. Therefore, your dog will begin to swing his head from side to side looking for the dummy. Too much of this will teach him to swim a slow zig-zag route instead of full-steam, straight ahead.

Don't overwork your dog in any one session. In this drill, that's an easy mistake to make.

Process—Steps in Training

Select a location where your dog will not have to swim more than 50 yards, and where you can hide your assistant and/or dummy launcher properly. Then heel your dog to a spot about 10 yards from the edge of the water. Have him sit facing where the dummy will fall. Go through your blind retrieve sequence, and as you say *Back*, "make a throw happen," that is, either push the transmitter button for the dummy launcher or signal to your assistant. Seeing the dummy in the air, your dog will run and jump into the water, and go after it.

Rerun it, but this time, delay the throw until your dog is almost to the edge of the water. If you wait any longer, he may balk and turn back. But if he sees a dummy fly just as he is losing heart, he'll jump in and go after it. Rerun it again, this time delaying the throw until your dog swims a few feet. Again, signal too soon rather than too late. If he turns around to come back before the dummy flies, he won't see it. Continue these reruns, each time delaying the throw a little longer, until he is swimming at least halfway there before you signal for a throw. If he tires before you get him that far, hang it up for the session and complete it next time. (In the diagram, the numbers, "#1," "#2," "#3," and so on, indicate approximately where the dog should be in successive reruns when you signal for the throw.)

The next session should be in a new location. On his initial run, delay the throw until he swims a few feet. Then rerun several times, each time delaying the throw longer. Thereafter, in each subsequent session (always in different locations), on the initial run, delay the throw a little longer than you did on the initial run of the previous session. Do this until your dog, on his initial run in each session, is swimming almost all the way there before you signal for a throw.

When you have reached that point, you should discontinue this drill, except for special purposes as needed. Begin planning your water blinds and running them normally.

Addenda

If not overdone, this drill introduces a retriever to water blinds as surely and as gently as possible. However, I don't recommend it on land. On land, the zig-zagging problem is greatly magnified, as the dog tries to see where the dummy will come from this time. Further, if the dummy lands in cover, the dog must hunt for it like a mark. In blind retrieves, that is a bad habit, one that should not be encouraged. (The above pop-up blind, which is similar to this thrown blind, avoids all these problems, so can be used on land.)

Appendix 1

Equipment

In the description of each drill, the necessary equipment is listed. Many of these items are used in several drills. Therefore, instead of describing them over and over there, I am describing all of them here in this Appendix, which you can use for reference as you go from drill to drill. In addition to the drill-specific items of equipment, I am also describing a few general pieces of equipment used throughout all phases of retriever training—whistles, lanyards, and so forth.

Belt Cord

This is a three- to four-foot length of stout cord with a loop on one end. It is useful in some of the preliminary drills (steadying and honoring). Ideally, you should make your belt cord from nylon, and burn both ends so they won't unravel. Attach the loop to your belt on your left side (assuming your dog heels on that side). To control your dog when he's sitting at heel, slip the other end of the belt cord under his strap collar and fold it back on itself. That way, you can restrain him with one hand by gripping the doubled-back end of the belt cord. When you release your grip, he can run right off of the belt cord, without even noticing that it's there. When you're not using it, you can wad your belt cord up and stuff it in your pocket, with the loop still attached to your belt.

A word of caution: If your dog's strap collar has a metal ring, do *not* slip the belt cord through it. If you do, as your dog departs, it may wrap up tightly around the metal ring. Twice retrievers have thusly removed important elements of my attire. Once my Chesapeake, Beaver, ripped a piece out of a pair of my bib overalls. Another time my Golden, Deuce, unzipped my jeans and pulled them partway off—when a woman in the training group was standing nearby. I don't know which of us was more embarrassed. Needless to say, I've never put a belt cord through a metal ring on a dog's collar since then.

Birds

You will sometimes need birds for training. Mostly, you can get by with pigeons, but occasionally you will want gamebirds (ducks and pheasants). For training purposes, birds come in three "conditions": dead; clipped-wing; and live flier.

You can re-use dead birds many times before they must be discarded. Simply keep them in a freezer between uses. When you need them, thaw them out, use them, and then toss them back into the freezer. Like many retriever trainers, I have a special freezer in the garage for frozen birds. In it I keep pigeons, ducks, pheasants, and quail.

Clipped-wings, or more simply "clips," are live birds with the flight feathers pulled from one wing only. If you pull them from both wings, the bird will still be able to fly away. But if you pull them from only one wing, you throw the bird out of balance so he can only flutter and flop around. Mostly you'll use pigeons as clips.

Live fliers, of course, are live birds capable of flight. Again, you will normally use pigeons, but sometimes gamebirds come in handy.

Unless you plan to maintain your own "flock," you need a reliable bird supplier, someone who will sell you a few at a time. If you belong to a local retriever club, some of the members can direct you to a bird supplier. If your area has no retriever club, contact the nearest spaniel or pointing dog club. They need many more birds than do retriever trainers, so they have to have suppliers. If all else fails, talk to your veterinarian, who may be able to tell you who in your area raises birds as a hobby or as a business.

Blank Pistol

In a training group, you need a blank pistol mostly when you are throwing for someone else's dog. In fact, each person in the group should have one. The ideal blank pistol is one that fires shotshell primers, which are much cheaper than .22 blank shells and just as loud. To fire shotshell primers, a pistol must be center-fire, not rim-fire. Most of those in use today are .32 or .38 blank pistols that have been converted to primer usage through the insertion of a brass sleeve into each cylinder. These brass sleeves reduce the cylinder size to that of shotshell primers. A .22 pistol cannot be converted to primer usage because it is rim-fire.

Of course, a .22 blank pistol with regular .22 blank shells will do everything the primer pistol will do, but the ammunition will cost more. If you already have a .22 blank pistol, use it instead of buying another pistol for primers. Otherwise you would have to shoot thousands of rounds before you would break even.

Don't be tempted by the inexpensive little pistols that shoot .22 "crimp" shells. These shells don't make enough noise to be heard at any distance. They may be adequate for training pointing dogs, which are always very close to the shot. But for retrievers, where the distance between the dog and the thrower can be substantial, they just don't have enough bang.

Calls, Duck and Pheasant

For hunt tests, you should accustom your dog to the sound of duck and pheasant calls. In hunt tests, hidden gunners use them to attract the dog's attention before throwing marks. (The sounds that come from some of these calls in tests would terrorize any duck within earshot!) For a duck call, use whatever you use for hunting, or whatever you can find at the local sporting goods store. If, like most, you don't call pheasants . . . what next, pheasant decoys? . . . and therefore don't have a pheasant call, check with your local sporting goods store.

Collars

In general, there are three types of collars: chain, strap, and electronic. The chain training collar, often misnamed the "choke" collar, is an obedience training tool, so will not be specifically needed for any drill in this book (although it's ideal for obedience, especially the *Heel* command).

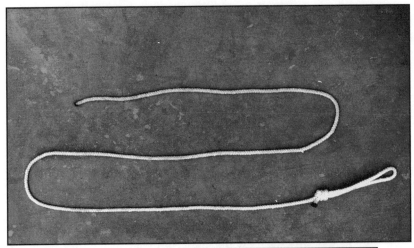

Above: Belt cord.

Right: Two blank pistols.

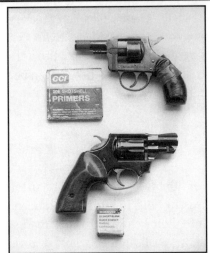

Below: Several duck calls.

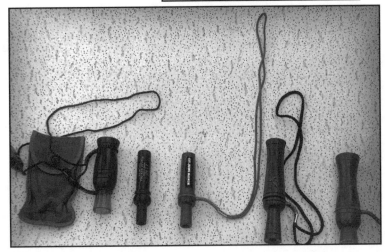

The strap collar has some usefulness in field work, especially during the steadying and honoring processes. (For this any flat strap collar will do, although leather doesn't work out too well for retrievers because of the water work.) Other than that, you should work your retriever without a collar, especially in water, where a collar can hang up on a snag and immobilize the dog.

The electronic collar (e-collar) is optional for some drills and necessary for others. If you prefer not to use an e-collar, you won't be able to use those drills for which it is necessary—unless you can invent another way to correct your dog immediately at a distance.

In Appendix II, you'll find all the information you need about e-collars and how to collar-condition your dog. Here I will only say that, if you

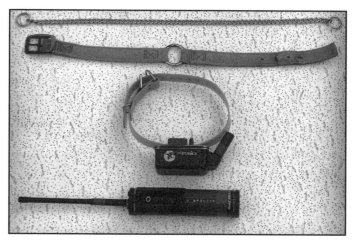

Three types of collars: top: chain training collar; middle: strap collar; bottom: electronic collar.

decide to get one, be sure to get one with variable levels of intensity, so you can adjust the amount of juice you give your dog to his particular tolerance level.

Dummies

You will need a goodly supply of dummies of one kind and another. The most generally useful are the small plastic knobbies. The white

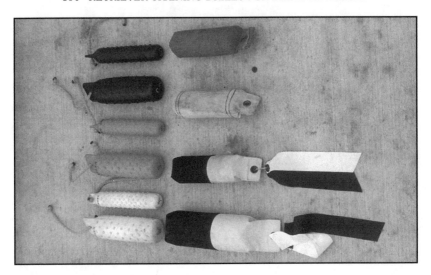

Assorted types of retrieving dummies.

ones are highly visible against dark backgrounds. The orange (or gray) ones are visible against light backgrounds. The black ones are visible against any background from light to medium dark. Frankly, the black ones are the most generally useful. In recent years, some companies have brought out two-tone, white and black, dummies that are visible against any background. The larger plastic knobbies also come in the same array of colors, and are useful in several situations.

Canvas dummies are also quite common. They come in a variety of sizes and colors. Some even have white and black ribbons on one end to simulate the flutter of a flying bird. I have many, many canvas dummies, and I use them, but not as often as I use the plastic knobbies. These latter can be thrown farther and more accurately, they retain their color better, and they generally last longer.

A word of caution: If you use canvas dummies, throw them away when they begin to deteriorate. I've seen more than one dog chew vigorously on rotting, leaking canvas dummies.

Lanyards

You will almost never see an experienced retriever trainer without a lanyard around his neck and two whistles dangling from said lanyard. I once saw a guy wearing his lanyard and whistles in an airport (and I have been

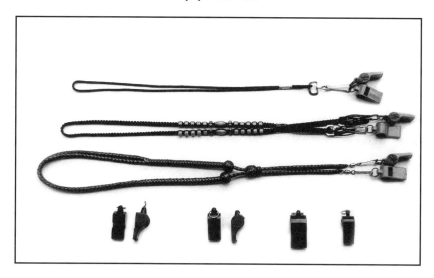

Assorted lanyards and whistles.

seen with mine in all sorts of places that have nothing to do with retriever training—grocery stores, restaurants, shopping malls, and so forth).

The lanyard keeps your whistles handy and free of the debris that can get into them if you carry them in your pocket. Lanyards come in many forms, from simple cords to elaborately braided leather affairs. In the psychedelic 1960s, and even into the mid-70s, retrieverites made a fad of wildly colored and heavily beaded macrame lanyards. Today, the more conservative braided leather type seems to be standard. Whatever your taste in lanyard design and construction, you should get one that accommodates two whistles—in case you blow the side out of one when you really need it. (If you didn't need a whistle at that moment, you wouldn't have blown the side out of one, would you?)

Leads

In general, three types of leads are useful to retriever trainers: slip-leads, standard four- to six-foot leads, and retractable leads.

The slip-lead is a length of rope or leather with a loop on each end. By running one end through the loop on the other end, you can make a makeshift collar for your dog. Using the loop on the other end as a handhold (like on a "normal" lead), you have a one-piece "traffic lead," which is ideal for heeling your dog to and from the line, and so forth. A

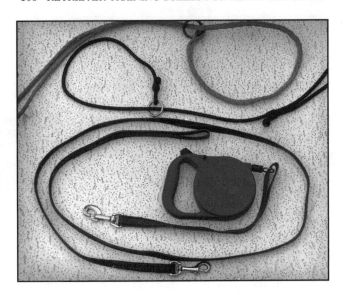

Four leads. At top, a slip-lead made from nylon rope; next, a slip-lead made of braided leather; next, a six-foot leather lead; within the six-foot lead is a retractable lead.

slip-lead needn't be longer than four feet, and many of them are three feet or less. Being rope or leather, it can be rolled up and stuffed in a pocket when not needed. Rope slip-leads are inexpensive, especially if you make them yourself (as I do) from nylon rope. Leather slip-leads, especially the braided ones with matching lanyards, are quite expensive. Frankly, I use these fancy leather ones only on spaniels and pointing dogs, because retrievers are too often wet when I want to put a slip-lead on them.

The standard four- to six-foot lead, made of webbing or strap leather, has a snap on one end and a hand-loop on the other. They are handy for many things—obedience training, "airing" your dog in public places, going for walks with your dog, and so on—so everyone should have one (and most of us have accumulated several over the years).

The retractable lead offers you a slick way to control your dog on a long line. It has an automatic reel that lets line out and brings it in as the dog goes away from and comes toward you. It has a button with which you can stop him and hold him at any fixed distance. It's chief benefit is that your dog seldom tangles the long line around his legs ... or yours. For retrievers, I use a large retractable lead, with about twenty-six feet of line.

Two different brands of two-way radios.   Gary Corbin looks through a range-finder.

Radios, Two-Way

Although not absolutely necessary, having radio communications with your throwers can be handy. Some dogs get spooky when the boss yells instructions to a thrower. With little two-way radios, you can speak in a normal voice and be heard at a great distance.

Range-Finder

To determine how far away a given mark or blind is, or to set one up at a given distance, you have three choices: estimate it, step it off, or use a range-finder. Most of us don't estimate too accurately. Stepping distances off takes time, and can't be done in water work. *Ergo*, if precise distances matter to you, you need a range-finder.

Remote Dummy Launchers—Single-Shot

In recent year, several firms have manufactured electronically-controlled remote launchers that will throw dummies or birds just like a human assistant (only more consistently). They look like huge sling-shots that use surgical tubing for power. Since they use a pouch for the "projectile," they can throw either dummies or birds. (I call them

Diane O'Hearne demonstrates the "Training Group" single-shot remote dummy launcher, which is made by Wahiakum Enterprises and operated remotely with Tri-Tronics electronics. Several other companies make similar machines, which are operated by various electronic devices. All such devices can launch either dummies or birds.

"dummy launchers" to distinguish them from the remote bird launchers described below.) This slingshot type launcher is a "single-shot" device, so must be reloaded for each throw. The resulting delay between runs can disrupt the rhythm of some drills.

However, if you must train alone, these launchers can be most helpful. You can set such a launcher up where your assistant would stand, bring your dog to the line, and impulse the launcher to throw the

Two makes of multi-shot remote dummy launchers. On the left is a four-shot "Bumper Boy," which is powered by .22 blank shells, operated remotely by Bumper Boy electronics, and has various warning sounds (duck call, shot, human voice, and so forth), plus a silhouette (of a young woman) which can be attached to the top to simulate a bird thrower. On the right is five-shot "Max 5000," which is powered by a mixture of gases and operated remotely by Tri-Tronics electronics. Either machine can launch multiple dummies without being reloaded each time, but neither can launch birds. Other firms make functionally similar units, powered various ways and operated remotely by various electronic devices.

dummy or bird by pushing on your transmitter button. By using two or three launchers controlled by the same transmitter, you can set up the same double and triple marks you can with two or three assistants to throw for you.

These remote launchers are quite expensive, but if you have to train alone, they may well be worth the price.

Remote Dummy Launchers—Multi-Shot

More recently, a few companies have produced multi-shot remote dummy launchers powered by blank shells or gas. These are small, platform-like devices on which you mount several dummies. With the transmitter, you can fire the dummies one at a time from a distance. This facilitates repetitive drilling, because you don't have to reload the

A remote bird launcher. This is a Tri-Tronics model, operated remotely by Tri-Tronics electronics. Several other firms make similar pieces of equipment, operated remotely by various electronics devices.

launcher after every retrieve. With two or three of them, you can set up the same double and triple marks you can set up with two or three assistants to throw for you, and you don't have to reload after every run.

These, too, are quite expensive. However, if you must train alone, they allow you to simulate a training group situation.

Remote Bird Launchers

Retriever trainers have also improvised with remote bird launchers developed long ago for pointing dog trainers. These are small, box-like, spring-loaded devices that flip a bird up in the air, but not too vigorously. Retriever trainers have made limited use of them, especially in the "pop-up" blind. Although cheaper than the Remote Dummy Launchers, described above, they "still ain't cheap."

More recently, some firms are producing more powerful remote bird launchers specifically for retrievers. These look much like the pointing breed launchers, but they throw the bird or dummy much farther. This makes them suitable for throwing marks.

Shotguns

Whenever you need a shotgun in any of these drills (normally for shooting fliers), use whatever weapon you use for waterfowl and/or upland gamebird hunting.

Sit-Stick

This is the canine name for what horse folks call a "riding crop." It is useful for correcting the dog when he is heeling improperly, when his line manners leave something to be desired, and so on. It is not specifically required in any drill in this book, but it is a handy tool to have around whenever you heel your dog off-lead.

The secret of using a sit-stick effectively is to pet your dog with it much more often than you correct him with it. If you use it only for corrections, he will fear it and shy away from it. If you pet him with it often, especially when he is sitting at heel, he won't learn to fear it, even after you correct him with it. If you decide to use a sit-stick, carry it with you constantly while training your dog and pet him with it—*a lot.*

Squirt Bottle

This is a plastic bottle with a small nozzle and trigger built into the cap. With it, you can send a stream of water into your dog's face when the occasion calls for it. I use one of these around home, mostly to teach and reinforce the *Hush* command when my dogs get noisy in their kennels. It is also useful in dealing with dogs that are noisy on the line while working.

You can buy these in several sizes at any lawn and garden store. I use the one-pint size, because it fits so nicely into one of the front bird pockets of my training vest.

On left, a white traffic cone visual aid; on right, a black and white flag visual aid elevated on a short orange stake; in the middle, three stakes (a tall orange one, a middle-sized orange one, and a tall white one).

Stakes

I use stakes in two colors, orange and white, and in a variety of sizes. Since dogs are color-blind, they don't notice orange stakes (unless they stand up too high above the cover). So I use orange stakes to mark blind retrieve dummy piles. That way, I know where the pile is, but my

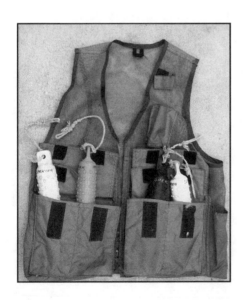

A training vest, with retrieving dummies inserted in some of the pockets to show where they are. In the back, this vest has a full-sized game bag. This vest was made by Wick. Other firms make similar vests.

dog doesn't. I also use orange stakes to elevate my visual aids when I use them in cover. I sometimes use white stakes as visual aids, especially when I want the dog to run for a distance before he sees it.

I make my stakes from inch and a quarter wood dowel and long guttering spikes. I drill a hole in one end of the stake, and drive the guttering spike into the hole. Then I cut off the head of the guttering spike so I can stick it into the ground easily. I also drill a somewhat larger hole in the other end of the stake, so I can stack them to make a taller stake when I need it. Also, to elevate my white and black flags above the cover, I stick the little "flag pole" into the hole in the top of a stake. I make my stakes in several lengths, from about 12 inches to about 36 inches.

Vest

When you train a retriever, you often must tote a lot of equipment—dummies and birds, collars and leads, blank pistols and shells, shotgun shells, the transmitter for electronic equipment (e-collar, remote dummy launchers), and so forth. For some strange reason, retriever trainers in general haven't yet figured out what spaniel and pointing dog trainers have known for decades, namely, that a multi-pocketed vest is ideal for hauling all this paraphernalia around.

I have long used an orange spaniel/birddog training vest for retriever training. It has pockets for everything I normally carry, with extra pockets left over most of the time. This vest frees up both of my hands and eliminates the need to drop things on the ground (and then search for them later). It also facilitates moving from place to place, like when lengthening a drill out or when throwing dummies for someone else in the "walking marks" drill.

I have encountered one very slight problem with it. When standing still for long periods, as in throwing dummies for someone else, I've found that bumblebees mistake my orange vest for a huge flower! They will home in on it from incredible distances. However, when they get close to me, they realize their mistake and leave. I've never had one sting me, or even light on me, but I have given any number of them a lot of exercise. To eliminate this distraction, my wife made me a blue denim vest patterned after my orange one. So far, the bumblebees have not "decoyed" to it like they did the orange one. If you train only retrievers, and want a vest, you should opt for a dull-colored one.

Visual Aids

In blind retrieve training, you will use visual aids to indicate to your dog where the dummy piles are. For many years, I used and advocated little white cones—orange traffic cones either painted white or covered with sleeves of white cloth. More recently, I've switched to little white and black flags. Other trainers use white plastic crates, white paint buckets, and heaven only knows what else. I've heard that a trainer in Colorado makes and uses little white "teepees" from three stakes and white cloth. They look like cones, but are much lighter and handier.

Whistles

You should have two identical whistles dangling from your lanyard, and they should be plastic rather than metal. In cold weather, metal whistles will freeze to your lips and then peel the skin off when you remove the whistle from your mouth. Some whistles have peas and some don't. Those with peas trill very nicely, but they freeze up and don't work in cold weather. For years I used the Roy Gonia (with a pea) in warm weather and the Fox (without a pea) in cold weather. Then the Gonia whistle came out in two configurations, one with and the other without a pea. I switched to the latter and use it year around. (Some more inventive types removed the pea from the old Gonias with a razor blade. I wasn't that bright.)

People tend to become emotional about their choice of whistles. When I started in retrievers, the Acme Thunderer was *the* whistle. Everyone who was anyone in retrievers used it, especially among the pros. I tried it, but didn't like it as well as I liked the Gonia, so I used the Gonia, and struggled to survive in an Acme Thunderer world. Today it's a Gonia world, and looking back I find it hard to believe that I received so much unsolicited advice about my poor choice of whistles. When my dogs messed up, I was told it wasn't a lack of training; no, it was that I wasn't using a "proper" Acme Thunderer whistle! Today the opposite might happen. If I were to wear anything but a Gonia, those given to offering unsolicited advice would attribute any problem I might have with a dog to the fact that I wasn't using a Gonia whistle.

The point is: Use the whistle you like best, and train your dog to respond to it, and all will be well with you.

Appendix 2

The Electronic Collar

For the typical beginner, the electronic collar, or e-collar, looms as something mysterious, intimidating, and more than a little controversial. Thus it deserves separate coverage in this Appendix. To de-mystify it, and to clarify its position in retriever training, let's review the following areas: the controversy surrounding it; what it can and cannot do; and how to introduce a dog to it. After studying all that information, you should be able to make an intelligent—and, I hope, unemotional—decision about whether to use the e-collar.

Let me start off by confessing that I strongly favor the *modern* e-collar when used with the *modern* training techniques which have been developed for it, principally by Jim Dobbs. More on both of these later.

The Controversy

The e-collar, which came into relatively widespread use in the 1960s, has been surrounded by controversy throughout its short history. And, like all controversies, this one has been highly emotional. Some proclaim the e-collar as the greatest single piece of training equipment in the history of dogdom. Others damn it as an instrument of torture, a device too brutal to be used on man's best friend. Most fall somewhere between these extremes.

Quite frankly, the early e-collars were crude affairs. They had only one level of stimulation: maximum. They had only one type of stimulation: continuous. And they were not too reliable. I'll probably never forget the nightmare I witnessed years ago when my training buddy's collar wouldn't turn off. His dog was on the other side of a small lake. He zapped the dog for some error or another, but when he let off on the button, the electricity did *not* stop—which was apparent from the way the poor dog contorted and wailed on the far shore. My buddy had to jump in his car, drive around the lake, and take the collar off his dog. All that time, I could hear the animal's pathetic howling, and I could see him writhing in agony. As I said, I'm not apt to forget that episode.

Nor am I apt to forget the dogs I saw back in the early days that were ruined by misuse of those early models. Because almost every pro used one, the e-collar became a status symbol among amateurs. Consequently, many clueless souls bought e-collars, proudly strapped them on their dogs, and used them in totally nonintelligent (= stupid) ways. Whenever the dog did anything even slightly wrong, the boss held the transmitter button down until he, the boss, felt vindicated. I saw dogs refuse to come out of their crates voluntarily. I saw dogs crawl on their bellies whenever they had the e-collar around their necks.

The Modern E-Collar

But why go on? The point is: I favor the *modern* e-collar in spite of what I have seen done with earlier models, especially by nonintelligent "trainers." I favor it because the *modern* e-collar differs radically from its predecessors, and because at least one *modern* training program for the e-collar is absolutely humane. True, improper use of even the best of modern e-collars will still ruin a dog. But today, anyone who will put in a little time and effort can learn how to use the e-collar in a program that is quite gentle, and much more effective than anything else currently available.

The major advancement in today's e-collars over the early ones is "variable levels of stimulation." The old collars had only the maximum level, which was a hefty jolt. Dogs, like people, vary in their sensitivity to electric shock, so in the early days of the e-collar many—in fact most—dogs were significantly overstimulated, day after day. Today, the trainer can select levels of stimulation that range from almost imperceptible to maximum. He can adjust the amount of juice he uses to the sensitivity of his particular dog. No dog need ever be stimulated beyond his tolerance level.

A second advancement in the modern collar is selectable "momentary" and "continuous" stimulation. In momentary mode, when the trainer pushes the button, the dog is stimulated for only an instant (perhaps a millisecond) no matter how long the trainer holds the button down. Many training situations are best handled with momentary stimulation. (In the drill descriptions of this book, whenever I recommend momentary stimulation, I say you should "nick" your dog with the e-collar.) In continuous mode, the dog is stimulated as long as the trainer holds the transmitter button down, up to a maximum of 10 seconds when an automatic cutoff takes over on most collars. (Would that my training buddy's collar had been so equipped that day he couldn't turn it off!) Many training situations are best handled with continuous stimulation. (In the drill descriptions of this book, whenever I recommend continuous stimulation, I say you should "zap" your dog with the e-collar.) Some collars have only one mode, either momentary or continuous. I would recommend a collar with both, but if you have a collar with only one, you can simulate the other mode fairly well. If yours is a momentary-only collar, you can push and release the transmitter button repeatedly and rapidly to simulate continuous stimulation. If you have a continuous-only collar, you can tap and release the transmitter button to simulate momentary stimulation. But these are make-do techniques. If possible, you should get a collar that allows you to select either mode as you need it.

Today's e-collars have several other optional features, most of which you can live without. Some have a "praise tone" button, which allows you to whisper sweet nothings in your dog's ear at a distance (after appropriate training in what this tone means). Having a good set of lungs, I'd rather yell "Good dog!" than spend the time it takes to teach the dog what this praise tone means. Some e-collars have a warning tone that sounds immediately before stimulation. Frankly, on the early high-voltage-only collars, this was a faltering first step toward variable stimulation. The theory was that, after regularly hearing this warning tone immediately before stimulation, the dog would react to the sound itself, and obey without being juiced, at least some of the time. That was a good idea when every push of the transmitter button lit the dog up like a Christmas tree, but variable stimulation has made it purposeless. This dinosaur may have a place in the Smithsonian, but not on modern e-collars. If it is automatic—incapable of being turned off—it's worse than useless, for it prevents you from determining the proper level of stimulation for your particular dog. At every stimulation level, he will react to the sound, so you won't be able to tell when he first notices the electricity. Frankly, I wouldn't have a collar with this feature, unless I could turn it off, and leave it off.

In summary, if you are planning to buy an e-collar, your first priority should be for variable levels of stimulation. Secondly, if possible, you should get a collar with selectable momentary and continuous stimulation modes. Beyond that, suit your fancy.

What the E-Collar Can Do

The e-collar allows you to send a negative message to your dog immediately at any reasonable distance. Since the timing of corrections is so critical in dog training, and since the distances in retriever training can be great, this tool fulfills a big need. No wonder pros persisted in using the early models, which had so many drawbacks!

But the e-collar is not a magic do-all training device. It has no special magic. As a matter of fact, it has only two uses.

First, the e-collar allows you to enforce *known* commands. If your dog is deliberately disobeying, especially at a distance, you can send him an "e-mail" correction immediately, while he is still in the act of disobeying. However, for this to be effective, he must understand what he should be doing. Thus, he must have already been trained to obey a given command before you can correct him for disobeying it with the e-collar. The advantage of the e-collar over, say, a swat with a newspaper or any other such correction, is that the e-collar "swats" him immediately even when he's beyond the reach of your newspaper.

Second, the e-collar enables you to create geographical "hot-spots" for your dog at a distance. A "hot-spot" is a place you want your dog to avoid. Dogs are highly place-conscious relative to punishment. They avoid places in which they have been punished. In fact, the more severely they have been punished in a place, the longer they avoid it. Thank heaven for this trait! Without it, I don't know how we would teach retrievers certain things, like switch-proofing, suction-proofing, angled water entries, and so forth. If your dog goes somewhere he shouldn't— like detouring to an island when he should swim straight past it—you can turn that island into a hot-spot by nicking him with the e-collar as soon as he lands on it. Then, on the rerun he will stay away from that island, and take the line you give him.

What the E-Collar Can *Not* Do

The e-collar is the finest long-distance correction and hot-spotting tool available today, but it is not a *training* tool. You cannot *teach* your dog anything with it. You must teach him through other methods. Only then can you use the e-collar to correct him for related disobedience.

If he doesn't know what he is supposed to do before you push the transmitter button, he won't know afterwards either. The only exception to that rule is hot-spotting. Keep that in mind, and you'll never abuse your dog with the e-collar.

Collar-Conditioning

Before you can use the e-collar for its primary purpose, namely, to re-enforce commands your dog already understands, you must "collar-condition" him. That means you must help him make the association between your commands and electricity from the collar. You can best do this in the backyard, with his basic obedience commands—*Sit, Heel, Come-in, Kennel,* and so on—which he already understands. (If you haven't obedience-trained him yet, neither of you is yet ready for the e-collar!) After making the proper association on several such commands, your dog will generalize the meaning of electricity. Then you can use the collar to re-enforce any command he understands.

Step 1: The Bark Collar

Although it isn't absolutely necessary, you should, if possible, first introduce your dog to electricity with an electronic bark collar. It will zap him whenever he barks. It won't take him long to figure out that he can stop the zapping by stopping the noise, and that he can prevent it altogether by being quiet when he feels like barking. That is a solid psychological foundation for "collar-conditioning," in which you teach him to turn off the juice by obeying a command and to prevent the juice by obeying promptly.

Starting out with a bark collar also works him through any trauma electricity may initially induce. He will learn to accept it as the normal result of barking. Thus he won't freak out when you first hit the transmitter button on the regular e-collar.

Frankly, there is one more reason for starting with the bark collar, although most trainers are reluctant to mention it. After being pre-conditioned with a bark collar, a dog won't vocalize when stimulated with the regular e-collar. Some dogs that haven't been pre-conditioned this way wail piteously at the slightest electrical impulse. Such a dog makes his trainer look like a monster even if he isn't overstimulating the beast. Let's face it: Some dogs are more prone to vocalize than others. It's in the genes. But we can overcome this particular gene with the bark collar.

Step 2: Determining the Proper Level of Stimulation

Before you can properly collar-condition your dog, you must determine his sensitivity to electricity. Dogs, like people, can tolerate varying degrees of shock. My wife is so sensitive to it that she is afraid to replace a burned-out light bulb. At the other extreme, I once knew a man who said that letting small currents flow through him relaxed him. He would stand for several seconds touching two electrically operated machines that gave him this sensation. I touched them accidentally once and jumped away at the first jolt of juice. Dogs also have different tolerances, and you should find the lowest level your dog clearly notices, the lowest level to which he reacts. He may twitch his ears or head. He may look surprised. He may glance around. But he will tell you in some way when you have found the lowest level he notices.

Put the e-collar on him and let him run around the backyard wearing it long enough so he no longer notices the additional weight. Now put him on lead, but not on command. Were he on command, he might not react noticeably when he should. Give him a continuous stimulation with the lowest level your collar offers. (If you have a momentary-only collar, tap the button repeatedly.) If he doesn't react in any way, move up to the next higher level, and so on, until he lets you know that he feels the electricity. That is his "base" level of stimulation. In some training situations, especially when he's either highly distracted or strongly determined to disobey, you may have to use a higher level to "communicate" with him. However, for most training, you should use his base level.

Step 3: Sit!

Having determined your dog's sensitivity to the e-collar, you can begin collar-conditioning him with his basic obedience commands. Start out with *Sit*. Put him on lead, wearing the e-collar. Let him move around near you. Then start continuous stimulation immediately *before* commanding *Sit*. Since he already understands the command, he will plop his posterior down. As soon as he does, discontinue stimulation, and praise him. You want him to learn that he can turn the juice off by

Collar-conditioning. Gary Corbin reinforces the *Sit* command with the e-collar. His dog is "Ben" (Benden's Xcalibur JH WC).

obeying. Thus, you hold the button down until he has obeyed, by sitting in this case. Why did you start stimulation before giving the command? Had you waited until afterwards, he might have thought he was being zapped for obeying the command. But with the electricity starting before the command, he won't misunderstand.

Repeat this several times, until he starts to sit when you start stimulation, even before you can say *Sit*. When he reacts that quickly, you know he understands how to turn the juice off. From then on, say *Sit* first, and only zap him when he is slow in responding. In subsequent training sessions, surprise him with the *Sit* command or the *Sit*-whistle—while he is heeling, while he is coming to you on command, even while he is romping around. Anytime he disobeys or even obeys too slowly, push the transmitter button and hold it down until he is sitting.

Within a few sessions, he will have mastered how to turn off—in fact, how to avoid—the electricity when you say *Sit* or blow the *Sit*-whistle. Then, you can move on to the next obedience command, *Come-in*.

Step 4: Come-in!

Follow the same procedure with this command. With him on lead and wearing the e-collar, put him on a *Sit-Stay* command and walk to the end of the (six-foot) lead. Start stimulation immediately before you toot the *Come-in* whistle. So far, in his mind, stimulation has always meant for him to *Sit*, so he may refuse to budge. To help him overcome this hang-up, pull him gently toward you with the lead, and sweet-talk him as he approaches. Turn off the juice as soon as he is moving toward you.

Repeat this several times, until he begins to get up when you start stimulation, without waiting for the command or whistle. Now he thinks stimulation means he should get up and start toward you. He may even think that it no longer means *Sit*. So you must disabuse him of that little misconception. Start mixing up the *Sit* and *Come-in* commands (or whistles) in each session. Whenever he disobeys either one, or is even slow in obeying, zap him with the e-collar. After a few sessions, he will figure out that electricity can mean either *Sit* or *Come-in*, whichever you happened to have said last. That is his first step toward generalizing the meaning of collar stimulation.

Step 5: Kennel!

Next, follow the same procedure with the command *Kennel!* For this, you can use either his kennel run or a crate. Start immediately in front of the gate or door. Initially, you should run a rope from your dog through the length of the run or crate and have an assistant at the far end hold the other end of the rope, ready to guide your dog with the rope as needed. Optionally, you can double the rope back around some fixed object behind the run or crate and handle the rope yourself. Start stimulation, then command *Kennel*. Your assistant, or you yourself, should then use the rope to guide your dog into the run or crate. As soon as he gets there, stop stimulation and praise him.

Repeat this until you no longer need the rope, that is, until he heads for his kennel or crate as soon as he feels stimulation. Thereafter, don't stimulate him unless he disobeys or is slow in obeying. Once he has the concept, start backing farther and farther away from the run or crate before telling him to *Kennel*.

Of course, to help him understand that electricity has no single fixed meaning, you should also work him on *Sit* and *Come-in* while you are going through the *Kennel* step. When he has mastered all three—*Sit, Come-in,* and *Kennel*—you have collar-conditioned him on three totally different, seemingly contradictory commands. You can correct him for disobedience to any of them with the e-collar, and he will

Collar-conditioning. Gary Corbin reinforces the *Come-in* command with the e-collar.

Collar-conditioning. Gary Corbin reinforces the *Kennel* command with the e-collar.

understand what he has to do to turn off the juice. At this point, your dog is "in balance," to use Jim Dobbs' term. With the proper command and appropriate stimulation, he will stop, go, or come. For all practical purposes, he has generalized his understanding of the meaning of e-collar stimulation, and you can proceed to use it to enforce any command at any reasonable distance.

Step 6: Et Cetera, Et Cetera, Et Cetera

However, for insurance, you should collar-condition your dog to other commands, too, for example, *Heel*. Follow the same steps as you have with *Sit*, *Come-in*, and *Kennel*. This will not only help your dog generalize collar stimulation, but it will help you get your dog from your vehicle to the line, or duck blind, in good order.

If you have already force-broken your dog, you should also introduce the e-collar to enforce *Fetch* and *Give*. This will give you a very solid basis for dealing with the three infamous mouth problems: hard-mouth, stickiness, and sloppy-mouth.

Step 7: Hot-Spotting

Technically, using the e-collar to create hot-spots (which the dog will avoid) requires no formal conditioning steps, beyond accustoming the dog to electricity with the electronic bark collar. However, in actual practice, you should *not* use your e-collar for hot-spotting before collar-conditioning him with the above procedure. If you intend to use the e-collar for both purposes, as most of us do, you should collar-condition him before using it for either purpose.

ADDENDA

The above approach to collar-conditioning—and the ways I suggest you use the e-collar throughout this book—follows the Dobbs' program, which I use and recommend. However, I should mention another program that is very popular today. I'll call it the "field trial program."

This program has been developed by highly successful field trial pros. Most dogs that are winning and placing in field trials today have achieved their success through this program. It is unequaled in its ability to instill field-trial precision in a retriever. In the hands of a cool-headed, experienced trainer who consistently reads dogs correctly, it is unbeatable. Thus, if you are such a trainer, and especially if you intend to compete in the major stakes at field trials, I recommend that you learn and use this program.

However, if you are not cool-headed, or not experienced, or not able to consistently read dogs correctly—in other words if you are the typical hunter and hunt-test participant for whom I'm writing this book—I recommend that you stick with the Dobbs' program.

In the field trial program, you don't use the lowest level of juice your dog notices. Instead you use the highest level he can tolerate without folding. Most who follow this program use the highest level their collars can put out. To offset this voltage, they use the e-collar much more sparingly than do those who follow the Dobbs' program. To minimize e-collar usage, they use several alternative techniques. Frequently, they handle their dogs (à la blind retrieve) to keep them on line to marks as well as blinds. Sometimes they use what they call "attrition," which means that they repeat disobeyed commands, thereby giving the dog additional chances to correct himself. Sometimes they use what they call "indirect pressure," in which they stop the dog, then before repeating the disobeyed command, they give him a "wake-up call" nick with the e-collar. And so on. Clearly, the trainer must be cool-headed, experienced, and capable of reading dogs accurately to make consistently appropriate decisions about when to use the e-collar and when to rely on one of these alternative techniques—and, for that matter, which one of those to use in any given situation.

For such a person, especially if he wants to win field trials, this program is unbeatable. However, since every push on the transmitter button gives the dog all the juice the collar is capable of delivering, every mistake is a serious mistake. And even the best field trial trainers occasionally misread a situation and "burn" their dogs when they shouldn't. Can you imagine how often the inexperienced trainer who seldom reads his dog correctly would burn his dog in error? Worse still, how about the hot-headed individual?

I've seen such amateurs—those who lack the prerequisite temperament, experience, and canine insight—abuse this program. It wasn't a pretty picture, believe me. That's why I cannot recommend it. On the other hand, if you make mistakes with the minimal juice used in the Dobbs' program, your mistakes will be small ones. Thus, I feel comfortable in recommending it. Granted, with the Dobbs' program, a person probably cannot achieve the same field trial precision that top pros achieve with the field trial program. But, who needs it? Hunters certainly don't. Hunt testers certainly *shouldn't*. If hunt tests ever so mimic field trials that participants must follow the field trial e-collar program, hunt tests will have failed in their primary purpose, namely, to provide an avenue where ordinary dog-owning hunters can succeed with their personally trained dogs.

Ergo, the people for whom I'm writing this book don't need the precision the field trial e-collar program offers. Nor are most of them capable of using such a high-risk program effectively.

Enough said.

Index of Drills

You'll want to read these, too . . .

Training Retrievers for Marshes and Meadows
James B. Spencer

Spencer's basic text on training for the amateur. A complete training manual that guides you step by step through:
- Getting acquainted with your puppy and starting him off right
- Basic obedience exercises every Retriever needs to know
- Teaching your dog single marked retrieves
- Training double marked retrieves
- Doing advanced marks and blinds
- Training your dog to do blind retrieves.

Softcover, ISBN 1-57779-007-3

Retriever Training Tests
James B. Spencer

The first book ever to concentrate on the environment the retriever must work in and how it affects the dog's training and work. Spencer explains which environmental factors are significant and why. Prepare you dog for successful hunting tests. Get this book today.

Softcover, ISBN 0-931866-95-2

Retriever Puppy Training
Clarice Rutherford and Cherylon Loveland

Is your retriever your house pet, and also your hunting companion? Yes, he can be both — the authors tell you how to raise your puppy successfully in this scenario. A unique feature is a section on the personality traits of retrievers and how to adjust your training accordingly.
- Select the right puppy
- What to do with your puppy between six and sixteen week of age
- Start early by making retrieving fun
- Learn lots of yard work exercises to do at home
- Beginning field work — when and how.

Softcover, ISBN 0-931866-38-3

Retriever Training Drills for Blind Retrieves Softcover, ISBN 1-57779-033-2
Retriever Training Drills for Marking Softcover, ISBN 1-57779-032-4

Look for these and other fine Alpine titles at your local bookseller, or you may order direct from the publisher at 1-800-777-7257 or by writing to Alpine Publications, P. O. Box 7027, Loveland, CO 80537. For the latest information and prices check our website: www.AlpinePub.com.